Shakespeare for the Intelligence Agent

Shakespeare for the Intelligence Agent

Toward Understanding Real Personalities

Yair Neuman

ROWMAN & LITTLEFIELD
Lanham • Boulder • New York • London

Published by Rowman & Littlefield
A wholly owned subsidiary of The Rowman & Littlefield Publishing Group, Inc.
4501 Forbes Boulevard, Suite 200, Lanham, Maryland 20706
www.rowman.com

Unit A, Whitacre Mews, 26-34 Stannary Street, London SE11 4AB

British Library Cataloguing in Publication Information Available

Library of Congress Cataloging-in-Publication Data Available

ISBN 978-1-4422-5677-4 (cloth : alk. paper)
ISBN 978-1-4422-5679-8 (pbk. : alk. paper)
ISBN 978-1-4422-5678-1 (electronic)

Printed in the United States of America

To Orna, for good old memories . . .

Contents

Acknowledgments

I would like to thank my dear old friend Michael Billig for writing the endorsement, Harvey (Haim) Hames and the anonymous reviewers for their constructive reading of the book, and Elsevier for their permission to reprint portions of my paper published in *Physics of Life Reviews*. I would also like to thank Hazel Bird for professionally editing my English; Molly White for her kind editorial work; and my friends Ismael Abu-Saad, Amos Elihay, and Saadia Gozlan for their continuous support.

Preface

What can man's wisdom
In the restoring his bereaved sense? (*King Lear*)

The idea of writing this book popped into my mind following a trauma from which I have not yet fully recovered but that provided me with an opportunity for mental and intellectual growth. Having worked for many years on various aspects of human psychology and personality, I found myself one day in a fragile situation in which my intellectual "habits," to use a Peircean term, were of no use as defense mechanisms. The metaphorical phrase that best describes this experience appears in the *Book of Ezekiel*, where the prophet describes the people of Israel as "naked and bare" (16:7), a metaphor that I psychologically interpret as an experience of fragility and the collapse of protective boundaries. In this context, I found myself one day watching *Caesar Must Die*, an award-winning film directed by the Taviani brothers (Volpi, 2012). The film is an artistic reimagining of Shakespeare's *Julius Caesar*, and I was struck by how insightful was Shakespeare in his observation of human personality and how rich is his literature in giving us insights into the complexity of human personality. The decision to write this book immediately followed.

The reader of this book may immediately sense a personal style of writing that, although evident in my previous books, is here much more connected with real life and emotions than are the somewhat abstract theorizations from which I have gained some of my academic reputation. The book aims to invite the reader to a challenging, enjoyable, and—in many cases—humorous reading of human personality through Shakespeare's plays. While the book presents strong arguments in favor of a novel approach to personality, it resists any dogmatization. Therefore, the theory presented in the first part of the book is not a dogma that aims to replace other dogmas but, to use a jazz metaphor, a structure that invites improvisation.

Introduction

For in much wisdom is much anger, and he that increaseth knowledge increaseth sorrow. (Ecclesiastes 1:18)

Disciplinary books in psychology are usually opened with a declaration of their loyalty to the "dogma" or doctrine of their field. Like Catholics, these disciplinary books manifest the idea that there are several well-defined criteria, both theoretical and stylistic, that one has to meet to be acknowledged as a true believer who deserves to enter Heaven. *Ipso facto*, one may easily conclude where the nonbelievers in the dogma are going to be sent.

In any case, this book does not aim to discipline the ignorant reader. The reader may know that the original meaning of the word "discipline" is related to physical punishment.[1] Indeed, accepting a dogma involves disciplining (i.e., punishing) those who might look astray. As my approach is diametrically opposed to this approach and its expression in intellectual life—i.e., life occupied with "thinking"—let me try another approach by opening this book with a *Gedankenexperiment* (i.e., a thought experiment).

Assume that you are recruited to work for an intelligence agency. Your job involves a deep, real-world understanding of human beings. You are asked to recruit people from another country for your organization at the risk that they will be exposed by their regime, tortured, and executed. To accomplish this mission, you should be a person with exceptional interpersonal capacities that allow you to identify potential assets; to understand your target's needs and weak spots; and to gain, manipulate, and maintain your target's trust and collaboration.

You should also be aware of the possibility that your work will not involve simple situations, of which you are in full control. This is not the safe context of the psychologist's clinic, where psychological authority is in full control.

While you are trying to recruit a specific person to work for your organization, you yourself might be the target of a counterintelligence activity that aims to expose you as an intelligence agent or to use your collaborator as a double agent for deception operations. As you now understand, you are situated in the real world, where *your understanding of other human beings may be a matter of life or death.* This is not the theoretical arena of name-calling, where the use of professional jargon to describe various aspects of human psychology may be satisfactory. This is not the academic arena where statistical factors extracted from self-reported psychological questionnaires constitute dimensions of personality at the *group* level of analysis. You have to deal with real individuals here and now and under the pressure of the good old reality principle, which has been forgotten by some of the spoiled children of postmodern, wealthy societies. You can praise yourself for gaining wonderful psychological insights. Your colleagues may admire you for your ability to conceptualize your patients' dynamics. Your case studies presented at the annual meetings of your professional society may gain plaudits for their exciting interpretations. However, these signs of success are mostly worthless when it comes to the thing we name "reality," a creature that lives its own life outside the clinic/laboratory of psychologists or the show business of the academy.

To accomplish your mission, you are offered an assistant and have to choose between two tutors. The first candidate is "J." J. is a young American Ivy League graduate who completed his PhD in psychology *summa cum laude* under the supervision of "A."—one of the field's leading gurus. J. has expertise in personality theory and experience working with the most popular model of personality, the five-factor model of personality (McCrae & Costa, 2013). He is also a qualified clinical psychologist, with a comprehensive understanding of the dynamic personality dimensions (e.g., Schizoid), personality disorders, and the DSM (*Diagnostic and Statistical Manual of Mental Disorders*) and ICD (International Classification of Diseases) criteria for diagnosis. He could recite from heart the criteria for diagnosing a person as suffering from a narcissistic personality disorder and has even published five papers in top-ranked journals of his field using an admired combination of sensitive qualitative methods and structural equation modeling.

The second person, let us call him "M." has a less impressive CV, at least in terms of academic expertise. He is a 75-year-old retired intelligence agent who is formally uneducated as during his childhood, his family had to flee from Poland when the Nazis came to power. When he was a child, his family wandered between several countries before settling in Paris.

Living in a family of working-class immigrants who made their living in the textile industry, he decided at the age of 14 to work as a deck boy, entering the United States as an illegal immigrant several years later. Warmly accepted by local bookies of Italian descent, who were quick to acknowledge his talent, he worked with them for several years until he was arrested by the FBI, which then used him as an undercover agent to break a network of illegal gambling at Atlantic city. Having had enough of the United States, he immigrated to Israel a couple of years later, where his next career began at the Israeli intelligence agency.

Now, choose between the two.

While the old agent probably lacks any formal or academic knowledge of human psychology—in general—and personality theory—in particular—and the young and energetic Ivy League graduate may be the rising star in his field, most likely, if you are working in real-life situations, you will chose old "M."

This is probably the correct choice, but for some people, it may be shocking. But consider: if one's academic expertise in human personality is of minor relevance to *real-world situations*—and I can describe numerous examples in addition to the one presented above—your "knowledge" is problematic, as theoretical scientific knowledge in psychology that is dissociated from the practice of life is irrelevant. To conduct a field operation, you would probably choose a qualified surgeon over a noneducated healer. To fix a car stuck on a highway 180 miles from Reno Nevada on a very hot summer's day, you would likely prefer a qualified mechanic over an amateur handyman. However, in the above example, you will choose old "M" over the expert, young Ivy League graduate. This conclusion deserves a serious discussion as it is far from trivial.

The idea that we have a "personality"—in the same way that we have DNA, lungs, or an anus—has gained indisputable acceptance in Western psychologically oriented culture. It seems that the ancient aphorism welcoming Greeks to the Temple of Apollo in Delphi—"Know thyself"—has been fully answered, at least in its modern psychological sense. Yes, we know ourselves! And our selves have personalities that can be described through a few dimensions. For instance, I am an extravert, open to experience, highly organized, agreeable, and emotionally stable. The genetic code of personality has been deciphered. Halleluiah!

According to this illustrative description, the complexity of personality can be reduced to the five "genes" of personality, as proposed by the current dogma of personality theory, the five-factor model of personality. However, is it really the case that the old maxim "Know thyself" has been fully addressed by modern psychology?

Answering this question in the negative is a risky move, while introducing an alternative is even riskier. People are usually not fond of critique, especially if it is constructive and proposes an alternative. Nevertheless, this is precisely what this book is all about. Not only that the book introduces the cognitive–biological roots of our personality, but also that—following the classic work of Vygotsky and Luria (1930)—it aims to show how the evolved complexity of personality and its daily practical manifestations can emerge from the entangled threads of the biological, the ontogenetic (i.e., developmental), and the cultural. It means that when studying the human mind, we should realize that it is a *synergetic* product of a natural history in which human beings are a part, of a personal growth process in which one matures from an infant to an adult, and of a cultural thread comprising meaning-making systems that mediate one's representation and activity in the world. Like the Borromean rings, the human mind cannot be broken apart without losing its unique and integrative structure (Neuman, 2014a). In other words, while naive reductionism seeks to identify the simple building blocks through which the behavior of the whole system can be explained, what we might call a mature "groundism" seeks to identify basic processes through which the *emergence* of complex behavior at the macro level can be *explained* as a synergetic product of the abovementioned threads.

However, this book's aim is not just to introduce another perspective of personality but to suggest that the understanding of real personalities *in vivo*, in real life outside the laboratory, may gain significant support through a close reading of literature. While psychology has traditionally considered literature as a surrogate of its theories—a field from which illustrative examples may be drawn, that may impress the audience with the scholar's rich intellectual background—here I would like to suggest a different perspective according to which our psychological understanding may be significantly enriched by reading certain pieces of literature that express their authors' deep, intuitive understanding of human nature in its culturally grounded and chaotic motion. To literary critics with a psychological interest, this idea may appear to be old news. Indeed, in the realm of human sciences in general, there seems to be nothing new under the sun. However, while we weave our *interpretations*, there is always a place for renewal and innovation. In this context, what is the logic underlying the idea that literature may contribute to our understanding of human personality?

When reading a thriller or a fantasy book, one realizes—whether consciously or unconsciously—that the novel has a structure, a certain type of "narrative." It has what the old-school psychologists, such as Frederic Bartlett, used to call a "scheme." However, the interesting thing about schemes is that they are more elusive than one may expect at first glance. Thinking about it from a different perspective, the schemes of the thriller, such as the schemes of personality, can be understood by an intelligent person in a very short period of time. However, and despite the simplicity of the schemes, the talented writers of good thrillers are extremely rare—as are the talented "readers" of personality. The reason is that, in practice, the *complexity of the concrete always overcomes the simplicity of the abstract*. By that I mean that our schemes, regardless of their indispensable importance as simple guiding maps, are no more than shadows representing the high dimensionality and dynamic complexity of the real world.

Those who try to understand human beings in practice by using the simple theories of personality—as presented in canonical psychological textbooks, or even in my own book—are similar to those who try to understand human beings by studying their shadows. While the study of low-dimensional projections may be highly important for certain tasks, such projections are too simple for our intelligence agent and in fact for everyone who would like to really understand human personality *in vivo*.

In this context, literature may play an important role in *mediating* between the messy reality and the simplicity of our schemes. In the more specific context of understanding other human beings, simple theories of personality are probably irrelevant in themselves, while literature—by introducing *laboratory experiments of human experience*—may help us to better sense the various logics in which human beings constitute and maintain their personas.

Given the arguments presented so far, the book is composed of two main parts, seemingly unrelated. In the first part, I present a perspective of personality according to which the grounds of what we call "personality" are threat-management and trust-management processes. I do not pretend to present *the* complete theory of personality but just one novel perspective that I found to be highly applicable as a guiding scheme for understanding real human beings, flesh and blood, neurons and society, in practical situations. This perspective has been presented in an academic paper (Neuman, 2014b) that produced interest and debate, and in retrospect even agony for some psychologists who are followers of the current dogma in personality theory (i.e., the five-factor model of personality). After all, challenging a "religious" dogma is always accompanied by negative emotions as the safe ground on which we stand starts to shake.

Nevertheless, my guiding perspective is empty without reading it into the mess of life. Here we come to the second part of the book, which is the reading of personalities through the sensitive, interpretative reading of literature, specifically through Shakespeare's great plays.[2] While the first part of the book introduces "structures" or "themes" that may help us to understand human personality, the second part is a *free improvisation on these themes* through the reading of Shakespeare's plays. Therefore, the second part of the book should be read similar to the way we listen to good jazz music, such as that played by Bill Evans, Thelonious Monk, or the Bad Plus. The link between the two parts of the book can be understood as one between simple structures and their free improvisation. However, let me just say that this improvisation draws on the themes presented in the first part of the book but also shows a strong inclination toward the psychodynamic perspective. After all, it was reading Freud that motivated me to study psychology at university, a motivation that somehow faded away when I met some of his jealous followers.

My belief in literature's importance in educating our minds can be explained by paraphrasing a beautiful metaphor proposed by Michael Holquist (1990). Do you remember Peter Pan? The flying hero from Neverland? In one of the movie's scenes, Pan is chasing after his shadow, which has escaped from him, just as if the shadow has an independent existence. Joining Pan in chasing and catching his naughty shadow, Wendy, one of the story's heroines, helps Pan by sewing his shadow back onto his body with a needle. And here comes my metaphor. *As in the case of Peter Pan's shadow, literature is the needle through which we may stitch the shadows of our abstract theories of personality to the messy and real-world life of human beings.* This perspective pays tribute both to our abstract theories and to the real and lived experiences of human beings with its full complexity. For our young intelligence agent, a deep, personal, and reflective reading of literature may be an important aspect of his education. It is important to emphasize that this is not the kind of reading that is common today in some departments of English literature, where decadence and politics reign. It is a solitary, personal, and reflective reading such as the one described in Robert Pirsig's seminal novel *Zen and the Art of Motorcycle Maintenance* (1974).

In this context, literature is neither the master of psychology nor its slave but the *needle* that is indispensable for weaving the threads of understanding. It is now time to move forward, first by presenting a novel perspective of personality that is the background for the second and interpretative part of the book. Let us enter our first chapter through the hole created by the needle.

NOTES

1. All etymological statements draw on the Online Etymology Dictionary (www. etymonline.com).

2. To avoid copyright issues, all references to Shakespeare's plays are taken from http://www.opensourceshakespeare.org.

Part I

WHAT SHOULD THE INTELLIGENCE AGENT LEARN ABOUT PERSONALITY?

Chapter One

On Baboons, Masks, and Character

Put off that mask of burning gold. (Yeats, 1994)

Our need to understand other human beings is almost self-explanatory. As social animals—and I have never met a nonsocial organism—we must interpret the moves of others and understand their "persona"—their *perceived* character and their *hidden* character. The need is therefore clear. When interacting with others, we must understand their interactive patterns of cognition (i.e., what they think), emotions (i.e., how they feel), and behavior (i.e., what they are doing). Being unable to understand other people might have detrimental consequences, as can be testified by old "M." We are faced with the challenge of understanding the other's character or personality but what do we really mean when we use the words "character" and "personality"? "Character" is an English word originally used to denote a "mark" or a sign. "Persona" is a Latin word describing the mask used by players in a theater. Are these terms somehow related? The idea of personality as a psychological concept is historically grounded in understanding the characters "played" by human beings, or *identifying the marks/signs that indicate humans' gross patterns of behavior.* In this context, the analogy between reading a text, or a string of characters, and reading a personality is clear. In both cases, we are dealing with the hermeneutic–interpretative activity of making sense of other human beings.

Other social animals, such as ants, can follow simple and straightforward "characters," indicating for instance the group's social roles and division of labor. The size of a baboon is a clear indication of his social status. If you are a male member of a group of baboons, you do not have to develop over-sophisticated theories of personality to understand who your leader is and to avoid messing with his females. In terms of understanding their leader's "personality," the most important cue is readily available for the baboons at a minimal processing cost, as a male's size is a simple and direct indication of his ability to physically beat his opponents.

In the current phase of their cultural development, human beings live in a more challenging environment than do baboons. For humans, basic "characters" are the building blocks of complex structures that are used for more than a simple signifying function. Bees may signal to other bees where a rich source of nectar can be found. A human being who is being informed about a metaphorical source of nectar, such as a rising stock, should always consider the possibility that the signaling "bee" is none other than a Bernie Madoff kind of con who is seeking to deceive him and to get his money. Therefore, understanding other human beings (i.e., reading their "character") is not a simple task.

ALL THE WORLD'S A STAGE?

"All the world's a stage," wrote Shakespeare, and we are players, living persona rehearsing a drama written by others. This philosophical idea may be warmly embraced by some models of personality; the paranoid personality, for instance, may be considered no more than a player rehearsing a drama according to which his deep conflict with trust is manifested. Following the same line of metaphorical reasoning, the paranoid personality is caged in its behavioral, emotional, and cognitive patterns in the same way that the actor is caged in his screenplay.

However, it was Michael Billig (1987) who qualified the famous Shakespearean metaphor and its implications for psychology by pointing to the fact that human beings are not simple players in a drama written by an unknown author. The players in the human drama have been arguing with their scriptwriter (i.e., God?) since antiquity and even reflectively doubt their status as actors. A true believer in the Shakespearean metaphor may argue in response that this complexity is in itself a part of the play and that we are genetically hardwired to believe that we are "free spirits." At this point, we reach a dead end, titled by the philosopher Emmanuel Kant "antinomy," where the two diametrically opposed poles cannot be resolved. As we cannot decide whether we are free spirits or marionettes playing in a theater of social norms and/or genetic mechanisms, the discussion seems to lead us nowhere. How can we advance our understanding of human personality if philosophy is of no use?

One of the heuristics we may apply to gain a better understanding of human "character," and the types with which this concept is concerned, involves examining both naive and theoretical conceptions of personality to see whether some interesting insights may be gained, specifically with regard to the underlying building blocks that constitute human personality. However, and before applying this heuristic, let us first dedicate a few more lines to clarifying the meaning of personality as a "mask."

Introductory books on personality use the term's etymology to point to the stable nature of "personality," which is taken to be a relatively fixed mask that mediates our interactions with both others and ourselves. However, this etymology/analogy may be interpreted in a totally different manner. In *Rabelais and His World*, Bakhtin (1984) argues that the mask is not a static configuration imposed on the person but is instead related to the transition, metamorphoses, and violation of natural boundaries. For example, in a carnival, masks may be used to traverse and violate natural boundaries between the sexes where men may be dressed like women and vice versa. Following this reading, we may think about the personalities not as "types" or rigid structures of human behavior, cognition, and emotion but as the *relatively stable patterns of dynamic transition that people apply in their interactions* with both themselves and others. The relevant analogy is the term "attractor," as used in the study of complex dynamic systems. An attractor is a certain location of the "phase space" (a multidimensional representation of the dynamic system) that is repeatedly visited. Only in pathological cases, which are almost by definition rare, do the metamorphoses of a person turn into a caricature, and such caricatures are indicative of a dynamics that has been *crystallized into a rigid structure*. Indeed, when we observe prototypal personalities in movies, for instance, they are usually presented as grotesque figures. Hannibal the Cannibal, the murderous psychiatrist from *The Silence of the Lambs* (Utt, Saxon, & Bozman, 1991), is a grotesque description of a "psychopath" in the same way as Pinkie Brown from Graham Greene's novel *Brighton Rock* (Greene, 1938/2004) is a caricature of a psychopath, and in the same way as Willy Wonka from *Charlie and the Chocolate Factory* (Grey, Zanuck, & Siegel, 2005) is a grotesque depiction of the "schizoid–schizotypal personality" (which is characterized by social problems and bizarre thoughts).

In fact, it seems that describing other people as having a certain "personality," rather than going through the process of performing a psychological diagnosis, is primarily an act of *social reification* that aims to solve the complexity of the metamorphosis that we experience (or observe in others) by turning it into a "digestible object" (i.e., a simple tag that we may use as a heuristic in deciphering the person). This is of course a powerful albeit a limited heuristic. For instance, Saddam Hussein—the late tyrant of Iraq—could have been described as a sadist in some reports of military intelligence profilers. However, without an understanding of this "mask" or personality as a process of metamorphosis in which a slum dog from the city of Tikrit in Iraq was turned into an Arab tyrant who dominated by fear, this personality title is of minor informative value. Knowing whether an Arab tyrant feels personal joy in causing pain to others seems to be of lesser importance than understanding that turning into a leader in an Arab country such as Iraq usually involves the transformation of the leader into a frightening man—one who may compete with the "sadistic" Judge Holden of Cormac McCarthy's *Blood Meridian* (McCarthy, 1992). Bashar al-Assad, who got his MD in the United Kingdom before becoming the leader of Syria, was presented as the perfect British gentleman but subsequently turned into the next Judge Holden of the region, sadistically repressing the uprising of his people. Our old intelligence agent—Mr. "M"—should have cooled down the enthusiasm that seemed to stem from some of the Western media when the young Syrian gentleman came to power, explaining to them that despite al-Assad's seemingly pleasant personality and acquired British manners, the transformation into a Judge Holden kind of personality was just around the corner.

In sum, describing personality as a mask is a limited analogy that should be interpreted in a dynamic way, emphasizing the transition that characterizes the person, specifically a transition that is associated with a certain conflict, as will be explained later in this book. Let us conclude by recalling W. B. Yeats's famous poem "The Mask" (Yeats, 1994). The poem describes a man who asks his lover to remove her mask so he can really know her. The woman responds by pointing to the fact that *he fell in love with the mask*: "It was the mask engaged your mind." Putting aside this perverted form of falling in love, the poem engages us in reflection about the true nature of our self. Personality is therefore, and as realized by modern dynamic approaches (McWilliams, 2011, 2012), always about *transition* and *conflict*, and understanding personality in practice deals with these complexities in the social context where they gain meaning. Social context, it must be emphasized, is not used in this book in the sense of the neo-Marxists arena where the classes clash. My use of the term social context aims to describe the *space of interactions where meaning is formed through symbolic activity*. However, complexity should not precede simplicity, so let us go back to basics by mentioning an interesting figure who has not previously been mentioned in personality textbooks. This person—a British gentleman by the name of Edward Bach—will help us to identify gross patterns of personality and to initiate a discussion on what are the *basic* dimensions of human personality.

Chapter Two

Dr. Bach's Flower Remedies and the Complexity of Personality

Dr. Edward Bach (1886–1936), a British physician who developed herbal remedies for healing, grounded his approach in a fascinating typology of personalities. These personality types are here used to open a discussion on what is personality, and how to define it in order to understand the building blocks of personality.

A couple of years ago, I met an intelligent electrical engineer who worked in a senior position at a high-tech company. This man had adopted the hobby of "healing" people with Bach remedies. As a skeptical person, I was curious to understand the logic of the healing process, and I read some of Dr. Bach's books. To my surprise, I realized that Dr. Bach was an interesting and insightful person.

Dr. Bach was not a psychologist, according to the modern use of the term, but a physician who struggled to find cures for his patients by using herbal remedies in a period when modern medicine had just started to take its first steps. From a critical scientific perspective, it is easy to dismiss Dr. Bach and his work as nonscientific mumbo-jumbo. However, reading Bach, I felt great empathy with this person who struggled to heal his patients, and found some of his psychological insights to be of great value, despite the fact that the effectiveness of his flower remedies has been scientifically refuted.

The fact that people still use Bach remedies may be explained by the psychological aspect of his theory and by the fact that he did not consider the sick subject as a defected biochemical engine. Rather, he explained disease through a deep connection between *personality type* (or what he described as a "state"), *disease*, and *healing*. This approach is appealing to potential patients, who may wish to be considered as whole individuals rather than as mechanical machines in need of repair. According to Bach, "disease is in essence the

7

result of a *conflict* between Soul and Mind" (1931, p. 3), where soul is a term describing the "real self" and mind or "personality" is used to describe how one perceives oneself as if from the outside. His thesis is therefore very similar to the thesis put forward by another British physician—Donald Winnicott—who became a psychologist, regarding the "true" versus the "false" self.

According to Winnicott (1960), "true self" describes the individual's authentic experience and "false self," the individual's defensive facade, mask, or persona. Here we have a *conflict between the mask and the underlying character* (the latter of which is, in itself, a sign to be interpreted as the reader will recall). Let us illustrate the conflict between the true and the false self by using the narcissistic personality. The narcissistic personality is mainly characterized by a false sense of self-grandeur. The narcissist conceives of himself as superior, special, unique, and better than others. This is a false self as the narcissist's *authentic* experience is actually of a weak and fragile self that can be easily cracked under minimal pressure. The true self of the narcissist is therefore in sharp contrast with his false-defensive facade. According to Winnicott and similarly Bach, the greater the gap between the true self and the false self, the greater is the person's pathology and suffering.

This source of agony and suffering seems to be simple to understand. In our social interactions, we may use certain ways of presenting our self—masks or personas—that fulfill a certain function. For instance, as a male competing for the attention of females, I may present myself like a peacock showing off its feathers. I may present a grandiose self that portrays me as a powerful male with a high social status. In the film *Catch Me if You Can* (Krane, Langsam, Lasoff, & Schain, 1989), Leonardo DiCaprio plays the role of the famous con artist and pretender, Frank Abagnale, who impersonated a pilot, a physician, and an attorney. All the figures he pretended to be were of a high social status. I am not familiar with any pretender who took the role of a plumber, a garbage cleaner, or a worker at a meat-packing factory.

In contrast with peacocks, or maybe not, human beings might deceptively present feathers that are *fata morgana*, an illusory deception formed for impression only. According to Bach and Winnicott, the conflict between my "real" self, whatever it means, and my illusory self, as presented to others, may cause some problems, specifically when the reality principle gets in our way. The reason for this conflict is far from trivial and deserves further reflection. A peacock that shows off its feathers but then loses in a fight with another peacock probably does not fall into a deep depression. I have never been a peacock's shrink but for me this is a reasonable conclusion. In contrast with peacocks, human beings may respond to a similar situation with depression. The "cognitive dissonance" between a false self and a true self seems to be of minor relevance for our peacock but may strongly affect a human being.

Both Bach and Winnicott assume some kind of aversion from an *incoherence* between the "real" and "false" self, but let us not take this argument for granted. As Billig (1987) has convincingly argued in the context of cognitive dissonance, people (like peacocks) can live very well with dissonance, otherwise politicians would have been inclined to suffer from major depression. The conflict underlying what is called cognitive dissonance, argues Billig, emerges whenever *we might be criticized for it.* This is a brilliant thesis; let me further explain it in the context of personality. No one criticizes the peacock for pretending to be more impressive than it is. However, a human being who presents himself as grandiose may be criticized by other human beings for presenting a false facade. This is a highly important point that *locates human personality and its conflicts in the social realm.* For example, those who criticize the narcissist for presenting a falsely grandiose self are those who construct the idea of narcissism to point out that in certain contexts and for certain people, it is inappropriate to present a self that poses a threat to the social status of others.

This is a highly important point. The dissonance identified by both Bach and Winnicott is a gap between the presented self and the "appropriate" self, which means that the "real" and "authentic" self is actually a self, formed by social norms rather than by an internal device. As I will argue later, what we call narcissism is a phenomenon organized around a threat to our status. On the individual level of analysis, a response to a threat to status may be in the form of self-transformation into an *Übermensch*, a superman kind of imagined self or persona. This move creates conflict, as others may be threatened by one's presented grandiosity. Here we can see how the cognitive-biological (i.e., threat to status) and the social perspectives are two intermingled threads. For example, Muhammad Ali, the famous boxer, said once, "I am the greatest. I said that even before I knew I was." Ali was known for his "showing off" and served as a role model for generations of "narcissistic" boxers who feel obliged to "show off" to gain recognition in a culture governed by mass media. If peacocks lived in a culture of mass media, we may hypothesize that they would behave like Ali. Now, Ali's strive for recognition could only have been accepted in a situation where there were no other competitors for the title. However, his narcissistic facade is constituted through the criticism of others who may feel devaluated by it and by his attempt to socially rise above his competitors. Personality is about conflict, and conflicts may appear whenever an outside perspective, *whether internalized or not*, negatively judges certain discrepancies to be inadequate. *The narcissistic facade is therefore an act of transformation that aims to move us up the ladder of the social hierarchy by presenting a self that is grandiose despite social norms that may criticize it for being as such. This constitutes a conflict as long as an outside perspective, or its internalized function, may conceive it as wrongdoing.*

We may conclude that personality involves a transformation to be interpreted. There is no sense in interpreting someone as a narcissist unless he or she is recognized as such. The transformation of the narcissist involves a move toward the presentation of a higher status, which is accompanied by devaluating others. The conflict that underlies personalities (McWilliams, 2011, 2012) is not solely an internal conflict but rather, following Billig, primarily a *social conflict* that has been internalized and has become a part of the individual's own self. This conception of personality locates it in between the biological, social, and psychological realms. I urge the reader to keep this important thesis in mind while reading the rest of the book.

Here is another example illustrating the social aspect of narcissism. We will see later how the conspirators against Caesar in *Julius Caesar* criticize him for being, in our modern terms, a narcissist. Caesar's persona is a metamorphosis that aims to increase his social status. Similar to Mohammad Ali, he presents himself as the greatest as he is competing for the title of the ruler of Rome. Caesar is criticized by those who are threatened by his narcissistic behavior. One may hardly find something that is *inherently* narcissist about Caesar, but there is a plenty of narcissism in the social context, where the threat to social status is a conflict that occupies Caesar and his competitors. In this context, whenever I use personality tags such as "narcissist," I use these simple tags for a communicative function only. These personality tags are simply nomenclature. In using them, I assume that the reader understands the complexity underlying them. Now let us return to Bach.

The conflict or the loss of harmony between mind and soul, as described by Bach, leads to illness that he advised could be healed through flower remedies. The logic behind the healing process involves a "holy trinity"—which is very easy to grasp—of personality, disease, and healing. According to this logic, human personality can be categorized into several types or, as Bach calls them, "states." Some sorts of personality *types* (i.e., discrete categories of personality) or *traits* (i.e., continuous dimensions of personality) are indicative of the *imbalance* that leads to illness. In other words, according to Bach, our personality is actually an indication of conflict, an idea that is in perfect harmony with the modern psychodynamic perspective, where personality may range on a spectrum from adaptive to severely disordered. For example, obsessive people who are normal and adaptive may be perfectionist, workaholics, or task-oriented individuals who put their emotions aside to complete their mission. Such a prototypical personality may be a highly successful surgeon who spends hours in the surgery room trying to save the life of his patients or . . . a successful hit man of the Mafia. In contrast, on the severely disordered part of this spectrum, perfectionism might turn out to be a constraining trait as nothing is ever good enough and, therefore, no task can be completed. The hard-working person who is fully dedicated to his work might be "caged" in his office for hours, at the loss of contact with the world outside, and the emotional constriction might be experienced as a loss of emotions that drains the joy from life and denies a basic sense of living. As we can see, the imbalance in the person's tendency to be organized might be a source of problems, and current conceptions—such as the cognitive-behavioral approach proposed by Aaron Beck (1979)—clearly represent the idea of psychological pathology as some kind of imbalance.

Bach identified 38 states that can be healed through corresponding flower remedies, aiming to return harmony to the individual's life. Some of these states are *strikingly similar to modern personality types*. This similarity may be used as proof of the existence of universal personality structures. However, this similarity cannot simply be used as evidence for universal personality types but just as evidence that the dynamics and constraints shared by human beings may generate similar structures. As human beings, we may address the same challenges as each other, and what we call "personality" may be the higher level conceptualization of the underlying processes through which we address these challenges.

Let us illustrate one of Bach's "personas." Under the title of "Loneliness," Bach (1933/1952, p. 16; emphasis mine) proposes the use of "water violet" for "those who in health or illness *like to be alone*." He also describes these people as very quiet and gentle. This description, fully elaborated under the title of "Loneliness," clearly adheres to our modern idea of the schizoid–schizotypal personality, as described by Westen, Shedler, Bradley, and DeFife (2012, p. 281), who refer to individuals who "lack close relationships and appear to have little need for human company or contact, often seeming detached or indifferent."

Another interesting personality type appears in *Heal Thyself* (Bach, 1931; emphasis mine), where Bach asks whether the reader is *"one of those who find it difficult to make decisions*; to form opinions when conflicting thoughts enter your mind so that it is hard to decide on the right course."* Here, Bach gives us a description of a personality type that is *indecisive*. This is someone who is addressed by the famous colloquial American-English expression "shit or get off the pot." This person's indecisiveness is a source of anxiety that can be treated with the "green Scleranthus of the cornfields," at least according to Dr. Bach.

The idea that an indecisive personality is a source of anxiety and illness that may be healed through a herbal remedy may be conceived as ridiculous to the modern scientifically oriented mind. However, in itself, the idea of an "indecisive personality" seems to be in line with our naive psychology and its corresponding theoretical concepts. We all know people who are clearly indecisive and beyond a specific context tend to occupy themselves and their environment with tortuous conflicts over the right course of action. In fact, they are paralyzed by their inability to act, and ruminate over their conflicts. These people are a source of suffering for their environment, and current Hebrew slang describes their pattern of interaction in terms of them "digging" into others' minds and torturing others with their never-ending ruminations.

The famous American director and actor Woody Allen has made a career playing a personality type, or more precisely a personality *prototype*, of an indecisive and ruminating intellectual. That is, Woody Allen may be considered the best example of the category of people who are indecisive. Being indecisive is another mask that may transform the individual. In Western modern societies, where there is a trend toward increasing female dominance, the antihero-like Woody Allen gains more and more credit as his masculinity does not pose a threat to the new social order. In fact, his character *is very decisive in being indecisive* and it pays well, as is evident in his success in attracting attractive women who in a totally different cultural context would consider his indecisiveness and wimpy character as signs of weakness to be avoided. Just think about Woody Allen as a young man in Sparta. Most likely, he would have been thrown off a cliff, as the Spartans allegedly used to do to wimpy kids. Here we can see an example of the three threads—the biological, the ontogenetic (i.e., developmental), and the cultural—proposed by Vygotsky and Luria in their seminal book *Ape, Primitive Man and Child* (1930). As we will learn later, there is a cognitive-biological base for Woody Allen's type of personality. However, as we mature in a modern society, we may learn that culture provides us with changing gender rules that drive some men to present an antiheroic and indecisive self. Woody Allen is a nice case that we may use to inject some complexity into naive images of evolutionary psychology. From an evolutionary perspective, Woody Allen is an anomaly as Mother Nature allegedly prefers tough guys such as the representation of the cowboy used in old advertisements for Marlboro cigarettes. However, Woody Allen's case teaches us that what Mother Nature really likes, if I may use the forbidden idea of "nature's intention," is not necessarily tough cowboys but adaptive people, and specifically those who are adaptive to the emergent complexities formed by historical social interactions.

We may now return to Dr. Bach and conclude that his success can be at least partially attributed to his use of personality types that intuitively appeal to our naive psychology. When introduced to one of these personality types, we may immediately recall a person who is an instance of it, in the same way as we may recall "chair" to be an instance of the furniture category, given of course that a chair exists in our culture. *Personality, as naively approached through descriptive terms, has an appeal because it instantiates personality prototypes that we are intuitively familiar with*. However, and here is a major point I would like to make, not every personality descriptive term (e.g., indecisive) should automatically be considered a basic personality trait and there is a need to identify the basis of different personality types, or better the general patterns of dynamics that generate these structures. The basic types of personality are not easy to define, in the same way as the basic emotions are nontrivial to define, because the criteria for what makes something "basic" are not fully agreed. The term "nerd," for example, as defined in a popular source of knowledge (i.e., Wikipedia) describes a person who is "overly intellectual, obsessive, or socially impaired." The prototype of this personality type, as described in Wikipedia, is Bill Gates. The term "nerd" is clearly a personality descriptive term. There are some people who we may describe as nerds and we can easily recognize a nerd based on our prototype. If you type "nerd" into Google images, you will find some amusing images representing this prototype.

In current Western culture, the term "nerd" is intuitively familiar to us, but we do not use it as a *basic* scientific psychological personality type/trait *despite* its intuitive appeal and potential informative value for understanding various forms of behavior. For instance, "diagnosing" a teenager as a nerd may be highly informative in predicting whether he will purchase a new zombies computer game rather than a new baseball bat. For a computer gaming company launching a new zombies computer game, the nerd "personality trait" may be more relevant/informative for identifying potential customers than other well-known personality traits. For this company and for this specific context, nerd may not only be a relevant personality trait but also be a *basic personality trait* (something that should not be reduced to simpler components). From the above example, we learn that the existence of a naive personality trait is not a guarantee of its inclusion as a scientific personality trait *despite* its potential informative value; therefore, we should clarify the criteria for turning a naive personality descriptive term into a scientifically established personality type, or more specifically, a *basic* personality type. It must be emphasized that, from a scientific pragmatic perspective, a personality trait is judged by its ability to explain/predict a certain behavior. This is the reason why certain "personality traits" discussed by astrology are dismissed from the perspective of modern science.

Since antiquity, astrological terms have been extensively used as personality *descriptive* and *explanatory* terms. For instance, people born between the end of November and the end of December are described as "Archers" and are considered to be adventurers and extraverts. As an Archer, I am a living instance that refutes this diagnosis of the Archer's personality. While the category of extravert is a well-known personality type, it has nothing to do with your date of birth.

The intuitive appeal of the Archer personality "type" is clear, as traits such as extraversion have been recognized since the days of Hippocrates. This intuitive appeal may explain why even today astrology is still used by some people despite the fact that it lacks any significant predictive ability, and therefore scientific value.

The use of a certain personality type or trait is justified only by its explanatory value as a hypothetical "mental construct" (a term explained below) for predicting the variability of certain behavioral, emotional, or cognitive markers in a given ecological context. Many potential cues can be used to predict variability in behavior. For example, socioeconomic status can successfully predict success on the Scholastic Aptitude Test; however, socioeconomic status is not a *mental construct* but a sociological *marker*. My mood may change as a result of the season; people might feel more depressed during the winter when there is less light. However, the season is not a mental construct despite its value in predicting the variability of mood.

Using the term "mental construct" seems, therefore, to be obligatory to differentiate between the theoretical construct of "personality" as used in psychology and other explanations of behavior such as biological (e.g., hormonal correlates of behavior) or sociological (e.g., socioeconomic status) markers.

WHAT ARE MENTAL CONSTRUCTS?

Let me now explain the meaning of the term "mental construct." Human beings—as well as nonhuman organisms—experience thoughts, emotions, and behavior through their ability to *monitor* and *regulate* their representations. In fact, the superego, a theoretical construct invented by Freud, is considered today (Holmes, 2011) to be the concept that represents these monitoring and regulating functions.

In Shakespeare's *Richard III*, there is a dialogue between two murderers who are sent to conduct a horrible act. One of the murderers has second thoughts:

> Faith, some certain dregs of conscience are yet within me.

However, he quickly overcomes this obstacle by saying:

> I'll not meddle with it: it is a dangerous thing: it
> makes a man coward: a man cannot steal, but it
> accuseth him; he cannot sear, but it cheques him;
> he cannot lie with his neighbour's wife, but it
> detects him: 'tis a blushing shamefast spirit that
> mutinies in a man's bosom; it fills one full of obstacles.

As we can see, the superego is a bothering issue as it "fills one full of obstacles." Indeed, when we become conscious of our thoughts, emotions, and actions, our behavior is *constrained* by our mental monitoring and control processes, albeit liberated in other important senses.

Having a direct access to our experience (i.e., the first-person perspective) is insufficient for our understanding of personality. For example, pain is a mental construct as it is subjectively measured through the subject's self-report and has a clear adaptive value in signaling acute trouble in one of the body's systems. When I am in pain, the pain is not only "presented" in my body but also represented in my brain, as expressed in the experience of monitoring and regulating this experience. I know that I am in pain, from first hand, and communicate my pain in an attempt to reduce it. However, pain cannot be considered a personality type.

Metarepresentations of one's mental and bodily states have clear neural correlates (e.g., Vogeley & Fink, 2003) and involve processes such as inner speech (Morin, 2011), which has been argued to be a necessary aspect of the brain's monitoring activity (Neuman & Nave, 2010). Inner speech is modeled after interactions with significant others, and therefore an important source of our monitoring and regulation activity—originally described by Freud as the superego—may be traced to social interactions with significant others who follow the norms of society—parents—as suggested by Freud. In other words, the psyche is mediated by the meaning-making forms provided by the culture in which we live, whether we are aware of them or not. In this context, what is described as the "first-person perspective" is actually the experience of the abovementioned metarepresentations, which are developmentally accompanied by inner speech.

When I feel toothache and report it to my dentist, this pain is "observed" and experienced exclusively by me. It is a metarepresentation (i.e., the representation of pain) to which I have exclusive access. Other people may feel empathy for my pain but no one can actually experience it as I do from the first-person perspective. Using the term "mental construct" is therefore our way to describe the first-person perspective or the metarepresentations that we use as part of our natural monitoring and regulation processes. It is a process, though it is accompanied by a later developmental phase in which it is mediated by inner speech.

In contrast with the first-person perspective, the second-person perspective involves the "mentalization" of the other's first-person perspective and is a phenomenon intensively studied in neuroscience. When I experience the toothache described above and someone observes me *empathetically*, he is actually mentalizing my first-person perspective. In fact, he is able to mentalize (i.e., model) my perspective by using various devices from mirror neurons to the interpretation of facial expressions and the use of cultural schemes that allow him to build a mental model of my experience with a clear predictive and behavioral value. For example, a mother who cannot successfully mentalize her infant's mental state cannot provide the infant with optimal care.

The fact that the first- and second-person perspectives exist is pretheoretically evident and scientifically grounded in our brain activity. These metarepresentations and their mentalization are mental constructs that have descriptive terms in natural language. When Jake describes himself as "joyful" and when other people describe him using the same term, they are actually representing their first- and second-person perspectives, respectively. Adhering to the first-person perspective does not mean that we adhere to the ultimate "authentic" experience, as believed by some philosophers (e.g., Husserl) and psychologists (e.g., Winnicott). As realized a long time ago by C. S. Peirce, when we observe our representations, we *inevitably* use the "mediation" of symbolic activity, as evident in inner speech. This argument should not be confused with cultural relativism or what is mistakenly interpreted as the Sapir–Whorf hypothesis (Neuman, 2014a): the idea that language somehow influences thought. My argument simply states that translating metarepresentations to communicative patterns, for others and for ourselves, is a process that makes extensive use of symbolic systems and therefore that beyond an elementary level of experience, our first-person perspective may gain form through the symbolic systems we are socialized to use.

It goes without saying that not every mental construct (e.g., pain) is a personality trait, but personality traits are *mental constructs* that seem to be relatively stable across time and context, and they concern our *interpersonal relations*. Being an extravert, open to experience, or suspicious is all about the interpersonal aspect of our life, whether we are human beings or baboons. Again, these are mental constructs, in the sense that they concern the first- and second-person perspectives, but with clear somatic and social grounding, meaning that they are mental constructs that on one hand can be grounded in certain biological structures and processes and on the other hand can be extended beyond the biological context through semiotic systems through which they are interpreted, monitored, and regulated. This approach covers both human and nonhuman organisms, but, for the context of human personality, I use the term "personality" to describe the (1) differentiated experiences of the first- and second-person perspectives that (2) concern our interpersonal relations, (3) can be grounded in neurobiological processes, (4) have a clear explanatory and predictive value for understanding behavior in practice, and (5) are extendable beyond the biological context in a non-trivial manner through the mediation of cultural–semiotic processes.

This description of personality seems to be too structural and might even be considered to be diametrically opposed to the social and dynamic perspectives that I have used so far. However, the reader should not mistake this book to be an "antistructuralist" essay of the kind, so admired by some postmodernist thinkers. As suggested before, this book should be read similar to the way we experience jazz music. I hold the perspective that personality structures can be found but I "play" these themes in a way in which complexity reigns. In this sense, this book rejects oversimplistic and dogmatic ideas of personality, such as those propagated by some proponents of the five-factor model, as well as some poststructuralist conceptions of personality that, similar to children in a temper tantrum, are more occupied with acting out their dissatisfaction than with telling us precisely what they want. With this roadmap, we can move to the next chapter, in which I describe the cognitive-biological roots of our personality. However, let us summarize what we have learned so far in few sentences. Through Bach's typology of personality, we have learned that there seem to be recurrent personality themes identified by various schools and thinkers. Personality, as I argue, is a term we use to describe certain "attractors" formed through the biological, psychological, and social dynamics in which human beings are involved. These attractors involve transitions and conflicts and are of clear social origin and cognitive-biological grounds. Therefore, studying them must take into account the three threads discussed by Vygotsky and Luria. The next chapter elaborates on a novel theorization of personality that is rooted in our cognitive-biological heritage but has sense and significance only if it is considered as one of the three threads.

Chapter Three

We Have Never Been Too Modern

The Cognitive-Biological Roots of Personality

This chapter is dedicated to developing a novel integrative theory of personality. It is argued that the personality types can be grounded in two basic threat- and trust-management systems. The theory presented in this chapter grounds personality in our cognitive–biological heritage while at the same time rejecting the "straw man" criticism, portraying it as a form of naive reductionism.

Let us start with the basic cognitive-biological aspect of our personality. In the real world, human and nonhuman organisms alike are facing continuous threat. I am not portraying a world in which Dawkins's selfish genes are violently competing with each other, leaving no place for cooperation, empathy, and mercy. I just state a simple fact of life that points to the necessity of dealing with threats. In cases where the threat is real (e.g., an approaching predator), we describe the affect associated with it as *fear*; however, if it is not real, but expected or imagined, we describe it as *anxiety*.

As a teenager, I used to jog in the orange fields of my hometown. It was a pleasant place for running until one of the dogs living nearby decided to join me—or, more accurately, to chase the foreigner who had invaded its territory. A dog that is chasing you is a real threat and the emotion accompanying such a threat is fear. Following this encounter and being familiar with the expected threat of this vicious creature, I felt anxious whenever I entered the orange fields. The expected threat resulted in anxiety that was highly functional, as it raised my awareness and arousal in terms of the possibility of encountering the potential threat. *Imagined* threats, though, are a totally different category, and it seems that our personality mainly concerns imagined threats.

Imagined threats seem to be unique to human beings and an inevitable result of humans' ability to *abstract*. One of the best illustrations of imagined threats appears in Stephen King's bestseller *It* (1980). Highbrow literature critics may show dissatisfaction whenever King's work is mentioned, but I find it to be highly interesting in understanding the anxieties of human beings. King is one of the greatest American storytellers and some of his short stories—such as "The Body" (King, 1983), which served as the basis for the wonderful movie *Stand by Me* (Evans & Sheinman, 1986)—have impressive psychological sensitivity. In his novel *It*, King describes a group of old friends who are struggling with an evil force that has been hunting them since childhood. This evil force has a unique form as it is described as an evil magic that can read one's mind and take the shape of one's fear.

This imaginary fear takes the shape of various figures but the most prominent figure is the clown. In one of the opening scenes, a child by the name of George Denbrough meets a circus clown. The clown's eyes remind him of "his mom's eyes." Is it significant that little George identifies a resemblance between the clown and his mother? I believe that this identified similarity has a deep psychodynamic meaning. However, I will not proceed deeper into this interpretation. The clown, who presents himself as "Pennywise the Dancing Clown," is not a usual clown but an evil force that pulls little George into the "terrible darkness"—toward his death. Fear of clowns is of course well documented, as something in the grotesque appearance of the clown can be monstrous and threatening. King's novel, however, reminds us how powerful is our imagination, to the level that it can form the realities of our innermost fears.

Although in this chapter we deal with the biological basis of our personality, the discussion of imaginary threats at this early phase of the discussion points out how deeply entangled are the biological and the cultural threads. While our ability to imagine is deeply grounded in our brain's ability to abstract, the forms of our imagination take shape in light of our meaning-making systems; while a child in the United States and a child in the Amazon may both experience imaginary fears, I doubt whether in both cases these fears would take the shape of Pennywise the Dancing Clown.

Another interesting aspect of an imaginary threat is that it may easily run out of control. It seems easier to control real or expected threats than an imagined threat and its associated anxiety. How is it that it is more difficult to control our mind with its associated anxiety than to control the fear associated with a real or expected threat? A possible answer is that a real or expected threat that is grounded in reality provides us with coordinates that may be used to monitor the threat and its associated fear. When the threat is gone, fear is gone, but how do we know that the imagined threat has gone? The answer is that we do not. An imaginary threat, like other abstract entities, is difficult to grasp and paradoxically seems to be highly influential.

One wonderful illustration of the dynamics of imaginary threat is a short story by Anton Chekhov, "The Death of a Government Clerk" (1999). A government clerk by the name of Ivan Dmitritch Tchervyakov is attending the theater when he suddenly sneezes during the show. "Peasants sneeze," as he says to himself, and therefore this impoliteness bothers our clerk, who looks around to see whether he has disturbed someone. Suddenly, he observes General Brizzhalov wiping his baldhead, and from this point, the idea that his sneeze had spattered on this highly ranked official drives our poor clerk crazy. The general seems to be indifferent to Ivan's apology, as he probably did not even notice the sneeze. However, the general's refusal to acknowledge Ivan's "crime" and to accept his apology drives our clerk to various oscillations in his imagination that end with his death. The imagination of Ivan Dmitritch Tchervyakov and the anxiety accompanying the imagined threat to his status as a respected person (not a peasant) are deadly. Interestingly, Ivan's imaginary threat is deeply associated with a process of social evaluation and his deepest fear is that he will be considered a peasant. From Chekhov, we may learn how deep are our imaginary fears that are rooted in the social realm.

In sum, we have described the need to deal with threats that can be real, expected, or imagined. Defensive responses in the face of threat are usually described in terms of the three general concepts of *freezing*, *fleeing*, or *fighting*, though the actual response may involve a mixture of the three. A flight response involves proactive distancing from the threat. This response is not highly appreciated in modern civilization although, as an old Arab–Palestinian proverb says, "fleeing is two-thirds of courage." Indeed, sometimes it takes courage to just run for your life. The fight response involves a proactive move toward annihilating the threat by attacking its source. When we describe courage, we usually consider situations in which people actively overcome their fear by directly facing the threat, specifically a human threat or the threat of predation by an animal. Courage, at least in the West, has usually been described in the context of the battlefield, where the brave soldier fights his opponent. In this context, we may understand why a fight response characterizes Shakespeare's brave generals, from Othello to Macbeth, as it is associated with a specific kind of threat from other human beings.

The praise of courage that is applicable to the battlefield is not universal, as different cultures think differently about the meaning of courage. A noticeable refutation of the battle kind of courage is a saying in one of Judaism's most important ethical texts—*The Sayings of the Fathers* (dated to approximately 200 CE)—in which a hero is described as someone who can control his urges. For Judaism, which has always been suspicious of kings and generals, real courage lies in coping with one's *own* urges and desires. The threat identified by the Jewish scholars comes from within.

Among human beings, the fight response can take the form of an abstract symbolic activity and can be associated with defense mechanisms, such as "projection," where the aggressive intentions of the subject are attributed to others. In other words, we can consider projection as the abstraction of a fight response. This is of course not a parallel of a fight response but a defense mechanism grounded in a fight response. For instance, the paranoid personality is described in the psychodynamic literature as using the defense mechanism of projection. Here is where the biological and the cultural threads merge. We share the fight response with many other organisms, but abstracting the fight response into projection is a unique human activity. It is also an activity that involves cultural variations.

In some cultural meaning-making systems, it is normative and legitimate to respond to an imagined threat through projections. *The Protocols of the Elderly of Zion* is an anti-Semitic document, in which the invented and imagined threat of the Jews may be interpreted as the expression of projection. In this text, the Jews are paranoidically described as involved in an orchestrated and secret conspiracy to govern the world.

Interestingly, at the cultural level of analysis, projection can be identified whenever the threat

1. is unequally distributed among potential offenders; and
2. lacks an empirically grounded risk-assessment procedure.

For instance, a close analysis of the anti-Israeli boycott movements illustrates the aforementioned dynamics and criteria. While Israel is portrayed as the ultimate devil by these movements, there is a total ignorance of other states that according to exactly the *same* criteria should compete for the title of the ultimate villain. For example, China occupied Tibet and brutally oppressed its native population; Russia has occupied Ukraine and is still governing the "occupied territories" of Crimea; Great Britain still possesses its settlements/colonies on the Falkland Islands, near Argentina, and supports its "settlers" in North Ireland; and Iran is an Islamic tyranny where homosexuals are executed. These countries are not threatened with boycotts; the state of Israel is the sole and only focus of interest. Is there an explanation for this unequal distribution of hate and fight response against an imaginary threat other than psychological projection?

The *freezing* response is somehow in between escaping and fighting and it involves the halt of movement to vanish from the predator's scope. The freeze response also seems to underlie the basic defense mechanism of "dissociation." This defense mechanism, evident for instance in traumatic situations such as those resulting in posttraumatic stress disorder, involves the idea that "I'm not here!" The freezing animal attempts to escape from the landscape of an approaching predator by turning itself into an invisible static object. It "vanishes" into the background. In comparison, the dissociating person seems to "vanish" out of the situation by *disembodying* himself and experiencing the situation from the outside. He sometimes even experiences a kind of out-of-body experience and total alienation from the stressful situation. Later we will see how Brutus, the hero of *Julius Caesar*, experiences a kind of dissociation/ freezing that is in line with his "obsessive" personality. More accurately, the freezing response is one of the dimensions that define the obsessive personality, which is occupied by a transformation from helplessness to control and from disorder to order.

The three aforementioned responses are not automatically produced in complex organisms such as human beings. It is hypothesized that they are preceded by processes of *risk analysis* (or more accurately risk interpretation) that involve activities of detection and analysis of threat stimuli and the assessment of the *situation* in which the threat is encountered (Blanchard, Griebel, Pobbe, & Blanchard 2011).

For example, let us take the paranoid personality, which is usually portrayed as occupied with trust issues. This personality may be considered to be involved in a specific type of threat assessment, where a very high level of risk may be attributed to others as the risk-detection process has a very low threshold for identifying signs of threat. Therefore, we may hypothesize that the paranoid personality may result from biased strategies of risk management that usually decrease the threshold for detecting threat signals and, as a result, increase the probability of false alarms. For the paranoid, everyone is guilty until proven otherwise.

The paranoid, however, is not simply suspicious but has a conflict over trust (McWilliams, 2011, 2012) that leads him to suspect some people while expressing uncritical trust in others. The zealous followers of conspiracy theories are extremely suspicious of any commonsense or scientific explanation but may completely trust all form of nonsense published in less rigorous outlets. This is clearly an incoherent approach; how is it possible not to trust any reasonable explanation while at the same time trusting all kinds of unreasonable rubbish? The proof is in the pudding, and the psychological explanation for this incoherent approach should be sought in the dynamics that produce this situation. Therefore, we may also hypothesize that at the individual level of analysis, the *oscillation* between extreme values of trust and distrust that characterizes the paranoid may result from difficulties in *regulating* the process of risk assessment and maintaining a *negative feedback loop* that keeps the risk assessment within reasonable boundaries of cost and effect, which is the adaptive explanation of personality.

That is, the adaptive sense of personality involves applying a cost–benefit analysis to copying strategies; a person should be vigilant and sensitive to cues of threat, whether real or imagined/expected. However, *when the cost of vigilance is higher than the actual benefit of vigilance, the person's behavior crystallizes into the paranoid "persona" familiar to us from the clinical literature and is described as nonadaptive.*

This explanation is generally enough to explain even the delicate nuances of human behavior. For instance, as an undergraduate student of psychology, I met a detective who told me that the higher ranked criminals he had met in his work were extremely "paranoid," and trusted no one. Indeed, the head of the Sicilian Mafia may be considered paranoid as he is highly vigilant and suspicious. However, this is a *highly adaptive* form of suspicion as the price that the criminal might pay for a mistake in trusting others is death. In this context, using the term "paranoid" may be inadequate and practically irrelevant when forensically profiling these people.

In contrast with the rational form of "paranoia" expressed by the godfather of the Sicilian Mafia, the ultimate paranoid—who suspects everyone—cannot maintain adaptive behavior as trust is a necessary aspect of social life. Even the Mafia's godfather or a dictator such as Stalin must maintain some kind of trust system. Therefore, the "overdeveloped" vigilance and suspicion of the paranoid personality disorder is prone to running out of control, a dynamic that points to the impeded activity of a negative feedback loop that aims to keep the system's values within adaptive boundaries. "Paranoid" is therefore just a tag we may use as a heuristic move to describe those who deviate from our norms and values of suspicion; the real importance is in understanding the underlying dynamics in which the management of risk assessment is unregulated. This idea of personality as overdeveloped versus underdeveloped schemes has been powerfully presented of course by Beck (1979), but here I would like to ground these dynamics in a basic cognitive-biological process involving threat and trust management.

Following the aforementioned line of theorization that naturally leads to the hypothesis that the defense mechanism of the paranoid personality, which involves an *attack* on potential offenders, may result from the combination of assessing threat and assessing situation, where the risk is assessed as high and the situation as such that it cannot support the response of freezing or fleeing. Assessing the situation, therefore, involves an attempt to understand *how supportive the context is* in different types of response to the threat.

Fighting back may not necessarily be the default and therefore assessing the *situation* is a must to determine the best response to the threat. A nice joke that I heard many years ago when practicing karate as a teenager was about a short and thin Japanese karate master who attended a bar in Texas. The guy who told us the joke proceeded by describing a situation in which several huge Texan guys approached the thin master while he was peacefully drinking at the bar and started to harass him. The Japanese master slowly turned to these huge guys, being ready to teach them a lesson. Then the guy stopped telling us the joke and asked a seemingly rhetorical question, "And now, can you guess what happened?" He immediately answered his own question: "They kicked the living shit out of him!" The humorous punch line of the joke results from violating our expectation that the thin Japanese master will teach the bad guys a lesson, as we have often seen in kung fu and American action movies. However, in real-life situations, it is usually better to avoid a fight response targeted against huge guys in a Texan bar even if you are a master in karate. Even if the risk is high, assessing the situation is highly important in determining the right course of action.

Let us continue our theorization by sticking to the paranoid personality. The paranoid personality attributes a high risk to other people who are conceived as holding aggressive and exploitive intentions. The threat is therefore *imagined*. Paranoid individuals also conceive of the situation as leaving no place for escape; a phrase that epitomizes this conceptualization is "with my back against the wall." There is no place for any response other than fighting back. In sum, instead of accepting the paranoid personality as a top–down conceptualization per se, we may describe it as a coping style that is phenomenologically (i.e., as experienced from the individual's first-person perspective) occupied by a conflict over trust and that is grounded in a unique context of risk assessment and the combination of a perceived threat and situation leading to a fighting defense against the imagined threat of aggressive others.

Following this line of reasoning, the paranoid personality may be better understood by additionally taking into account the fact that organisms occasionally have to face high-consequence events. Such an event may be a once-in-a-lifetime struggle for life. This kind of event may be extremely rare from a statistical point of view but have significant consequences. Think for instance about the secret service agents who protect the president of a country. Attempts to shoot a president are statistically rare. The probability that an agent will experience such an event is extremely low. However, the consequences of such a rare event have a high price and, therefore, one should be prepared for such a low-probability event.

Woody and Szechtman (2011) suggest that, to address the abovementioned challenge, organisms are equipped with a "security motivation system," which is an independent module in the brain. Characterizing this system, they suggest that organisms risk assessment draws on subtle and indirect cues (Woody & Szechtman, 2011, p. 1020). These are not signals of a clear danger, such as the exposed teeth of an aggressive predator, but "petite signs" that must be carefully interpreted. In this context, another point raised by the researchers is that the animal's vigilance is activated by relatively weak cues. This means that the system's susceptibility to alerts is such that there will be a high proportion of false alarms. The third point these authors discuss is the probing and manipulation of the environment to acquire further information regarding potential risks, which means that the organism is *proactive* in identifying signs of threat. A paranoid is someone who not only is hypervigilant and attuned to subtle and uncertain cues of threat from others but also probes the environment (e.g., reading about conspiracy theories) for cues of danger and has a risk-management strategy that involves a disproportionate level of false alarms.

In sum, adopting the threat- and risk-management perspectives, we may characterize the paranoid personality as a vigilant and highly sensitive cue-detecting system that attributes high risk to potential threats from others, evaluates situations as not allowing freeze or escape, and therefore performs preventive attack as a defense strategy. Moreover, it is a unique persona characterized by a specific form of transition or dynamics between the two poles of trust and distrust. The specific nature of the paranoid threat and trust systems are culturally mediated, whether the alleged threat is a Central Intelligence Agency spy or Jews, identified through European blood libels as murderous creatures. The next sections delve deeper into the threat system to better associate it with higher order structures of personality.

TYPES OF THREAT

While threat detection may be a universal structure, the *exact nature of the threat* may significantly vary between species and situations. For instance, Boyer and Bergstrom (2011) detailed the dangers that humans have faced during their long evolutionary history. These dangers include predation, contagion and contamination, status threat, and conspecific violence from other humans.

The paranoid personality is threatened by an *imagined* conspecific violence or abstract form of predation. John Nash—a Noble laureate, whose life has been described in the film *A Beautiful Mind* (Grazer & Howard, 2001)—has been diagnosed as paranoid. As you may recall from the film, Nash's hallucinations involved the deep and painful idea that he was being *hunted* like an animal. If a person describes an imaginary fear in terms of *predation*, you may suspect that he is paranoid.

In contrast with the paranoid personality, what is known as the narcissistic personality is clearly threatened by *status*. Interesting supporting evidence gained from a neuroscience perspective is found in a paper by Cascio, Konrath, and Falk (2015). This study found that narcissism is associated with activity in an area related to a *social pain network* and suggests that hypersensitivity to exclusion in narcissists may be related to hypersensitivity in brain systems associated with this distress.

In contrast with the narcissistic personality, there are indications (e.g., Olatunji, Lohr, Sawchuk, & Tolin, 2007) that the obsessive personality is threatened by an abstract form of *contagion*. Think about the way obsessed people are occupied with the issue of cleanness and with controlling what should be inside or what should be outside their body.

It is argued by Neuberg, Kenrick, and Schaller (2011) that people have evolved two different management systems: one that involves *self-protection* and the other *disease avoidance*. The self-protection system involves the identification of harmful intentions by conspecifics through cues such as angry facial expressions, especially if the threatening subject is an outgroup male. Others may threaten the individual not only through direct violence but also through the transmission of a disease. Transmission of disease may be identified through abnormal bodily symptoms such as wounds and other things we may describe as "disgusting." This threat involves the danger of contagion, as presented before. In contrast to the self-protection system (which is characterized by a fearful emotional response), the disease-avoidance system is characterized by a rather different emotion: *disgust*. The avoidant personality may be nurtured by this threat; it has been shown that avoidance is a typical reaction to the threat of contagion (Neuberg et al., 2011). If a person might be infectious, the last thing one will want to do is touch him. Most people will want to stay, as far as possible, away from him.

Identifying the source of the imaginary threat occupying a certain person and that person's unique dynamics may help us to understand his personality. For instance, while the paranoid is certain that others plan to initiate violent attacks against him, the obsessive–compulsive personality is ambivalent about the cues that he interprets: is it a nurturing "food" to be consumed or a poisonous "food" to be avoided or thrown out? In this sense, the obsessive is occupied with "stimuli that one needs or desires to approach but that also contain potential threat (thus creating an approach avoidance conflict)." These threats "activate the behavioral inhibition system [avoidance system], which produces vigilance, rumination, and passive avoidance, as well as anxiety and even potentially depression" (Gray & McNaughton cited in DeYoung & Gray, 2009, p. 324).

At this point, we may better understand the indecisive nature of the "anal" personality, which is both *attracted to and disgusted by* a certain source of pleasure. If you know people obsessed by cleaning, then you know that they are both attracted to and disgusted by dirt. The obsessive, anal personality is indecisive and paralyzed, ruminating over the right course of action while unable to make a decision. When he makes a decision, it is usually a fight response, such as launching a war against each and every single germ populating a toilet. Therefore, the main defense mechanisms of the obsessive personality are *freeze* and *fight*. The dynamics characterizing

Table 3.1. A comparison between the paranoid and the obsessive–compulsive personality types

Personality Type	Paranoid	Obsessive–Compulsive
Assessed risk/source	High/attack	Uncertain/contagion
Assessed situation	Does not flee/freeze	Does not attack/flee
Major defensive response	Fight/projection	Freeze/avoidance
Affect	Rage	Disgust

this personality consist of a rigid and limited negative feedback loop that restricts the individual's scope to a well-defined set of behaviors and rituals of *control*. The hypothetical differences between the paranoid and obsessive–compulsive personalities in terms of threat management are summarized in table 3.1.

It must be noted that the above cognitive-biological characterization of personality is *problem-oriented*. The problem that both the paranoid and the obsessed are addressing (as do nonhuman organisms) is threat management. In the first case, it is the imaginary threat associated with potential offenders, and in the second case, it is the threat of imaginary contagion.

It must also be emphasized that our minds have developed primarily to deal with threats. The olfactory system is just one case illustrating this point as it has developed to identify poisonous and potentially harmful foods rather than the pleasurable nuances of modern delicatessens. Analyzing personality from the perspective of threat and trust management may have interesting implications. For instance, both men and women are described in the literature through the same personality types and it seems reasonable that, because of the biological and evolutionarily grounded differences between males and females, these differences are expressed in terms of *qualitative* differences in personality. One context in which such differences are inevitable is the context of "sperm competition."

SPERM COMPETITION AND THE
POOR AMERICAN SOLDIERS

Sperm competition concerns the competitive process between the spermatozoa of two or more different males who have had sex with the same female at different times to fertilize an egg of that single female (Birkhead & Møller, 1998; Parker, 1970; Shackelford & Goetz, 2007; Shackelford, Pound & Goetz, 2005; Shackelford et al., 2002). Sperm competition is a source of threat and anxiety as the male can never fully trust the female to carry and fertilize his own sperm. This is probably one of the main underlying reasons for men's fear of cuckoldry, a fear that is a repeated theme in Shakespeare's plays, one example being *Much Ado About Nothing*. Interestingly, it is not usually included in the basic list of threats that humans have faced throughout their evolutionary history, probably because it is a threat that is specific to men. Sperm competition is a unique source of threat and anxiety that has no symmetry between the genders. This threat may risk not only the male's sperm but also, in the context of human organisms, the male's sense of manhood and his "face" (i.e., his positive social status). As presented by Shakespeare in *Much Ado About Nothing*, the threat of sperm competition is translated into the painful social embarrassment of the cheated husband who has been cuckolded. The expression "to furnish with horns" means to cuckold. The "horns," a word that is associated with "horny," suggest that the cheating wife has had sex with someone who is manlier than the cuckolded husband. As you remember, in many cultures, the devil himself is presented as a creature with horns. Now we can understand why the ultimate evil is portrayed as a "horny" fellow and that sperm competition is associated with raised suspicion toward other men and may interact with a paranoid dimension of personality.

In 2012, when the rate of suicide in the American army reached a peak, a lot of effort was put into trying to explain why so many men in service take their own life. The favorite explanation was posttraumatic stress disorder resulting from the soldiers' battle experience. The only problem with this explanation was that too many of those who committed suicide had not had the "pleasure" of experiencing a battlefield. However, in the imagination of the American media, and regardless of the empirical evidence, heroes returning from the battlefield have to pay the price, a romantic image that is groundless, at least as the ultimate explanation of the high suicide rates in the American army.

I have proposed another hypothesis. My hypothesis is that many of the men who committed suicide suffered from depression resulting from sperm competition. Serving in Hawaii or Alaska while their spouse is alone several thousand miles away might have driven them crazy. One only has to read Shakespeare's *Much Ado About Nothing* to understand how deeply rooted is this threat in men. I presented this explanation to an ex-colonel of the special forces, who was my guest at that time, and he confirmed that while serving in Iraq for several months, he had been extremely bothered, to say the least, about the loyalty of his wife back home in the American south. He got divorced after a while and remarried a woman who he conveyed to me was more trustworthy. It goes without saying that my proposal to study sperm competition as a source of depression among male soldiers in the American army has been rejected. It is much more appealing to conceive of ourselves in terms of the schemes produced in Hollywood than to look to the brutal schemes produced by nature, whether you believe it has a divine source or not. As I continuously argue, life has its own logic regardless of the fantasies we attempt to force on it.

While males may be concerned with sperm competition, females may be concerned with the risk of choosing a sick or uncaring mate (Watkins, DeBruine, Little, Feinberg, & Jones, 2012). This threat is much more related to the risk of *contagion*, as having a sick man as a spouse might have detrimental consequences for the woman and her babies. Therefore, while a biologically grounded theory of personality should adhere to the human need to address threats and their accompanying anxiety, as suggested by the psychodynamic and cognitive-behavioral approach, it must take into account various specificities that may guarantee its relevance to the analysis of behavior to include different personality facets for men and women. *The fact that major personality theories are indifferent to the differences between men and women is no less than a scandal.* The theory described in this book seems to do justice to this issue.

One potential hypothesis based on the above theorization of sperm competition is that some men who commit violent actions against their spouses may not only suspect them of dishonesty but also conceive the situation as inviting a conflict over a flee or attack response. In the first case, specifically where the male has a depressive personality and uses flight/introjection as a defense mechanism, he may blame himself and direct his rage against the self by committing suicide. A male introvert who experiences sperm competition is in greater danger of committing suicide. In the second case, where the man is an extravert, the attack might be directed against his spouse and/or the male suspected of cuckolding him. Where a mixture of strategies is evident, we may anticipate suicide–homicide. Indeed, Rosenbaum (1990) discovered what he described as "striking findings" that perpetrators of murder–suicide were mostly depressed (75 percent) men (95 percent), while perpetrators of homicide were not depressed and one-half were women.

This finding suggests that the combination of the threat of sperm competition and a "back against the wall" situation assessment may serve as a powerful predictor of murder–suicide. In other words, a man who suspects his wife, given the threat of sperm competition, might assess the situation as leaving no place for a solution. The combination of high-assessed risk (e.g., "she is surely cheating on me"), an assessed dead-end situation accompanied by deep grief (e.g., "I'm losing her forever and I can't do anything about it"), and an affective ingredient of rage that accompanies a fight response may together form a deadly recipe for murder–suicide.

What we have seen thus far is that a cognitive-biological approach to personality that is grounded in the real-world problems a person faces in his strategic management of threat may explain higher level personality structures encountered in the psychodynamic and cognitive-behavioral approaches, and, as will be illustrated later, in the five-factor model too. This approach relies neither on bottom-up statistical clustering of descriptive terms used by human beings nor on a top-down theoretical formulation per se. It is an approach that is problem centered (i.e., threat and trust management), that is shared with other nonhuman organisms, and that pays close attention to the unique particularities of the situation in the sense that the parameters of threat processing and response are determined not only by the organism's phenotypic traits but also by ad hoc decisions made in evaluating the situation at hand through available symbolic resources. Therefore, the approach can explain inter- and intraindividual differences as resulting from both "hardwired" and ad hoc evaluations of a situation. The next section further elaborates this idea by taking into account the second axis of personality, which is trust.

FROM THREAT TO TRUST

Caricaturists' descriptions of evolutionary theory sometimes present a world in which a struggle for survival overshadows all other dynamics. It is naive to ignore the violent aspect of life, which necessitates continuous involvement in threat assessment and risk analysis. However, for many social species, specifically for mammals like us, trust is a *complementary* and crucial aspect of life (Bateson, 1988). Therefore, trust is a complementary dimension to threat, and the second tenet constituting our personality. Personality with all of its variety involves threat- and trust-management systems.

As babies and infants, we are totally dependent on the protection and nurturing of our caregivers. In contrast with some species that are thrown into the world and that have to immediately stand on their feet, the human baby is a helpless creature that demands the support of his caregivers for a relatively long time. Therefore, the most basic experience of trust may be expressed through the complementary concept of *caring* (Davis & Panksepp, 2011), which involves nurturing, empathy, and in general the ability to care for those who need us. However, from an evolutionary developmental perspective, trust comes before caring because we must trust long before we are able to care for others.

A wonderful illustration of caring in one of its most sophisticated cultural expressions appears in a short story by the great American Jewish writer Bernard Malamud. The story, titled "Idiots First" (Malamud, 1963), is about a poor Jewish widower by the name of Mendel who realizes death, materialized in the character of someone by the name of "Ginzburg," is coming to take him. Mendel's last mission in this world is to raise some money that will allow him to send his mentally disabled son Isaac to Isaac's uncle in

California. In contrast with the Spartans, Mendel has no intention to throw his disabled son off a cliff. This is a clear moral–psychological stance that is of course grounded in Mendel's Jewish cultural beliefs.

Mendel is also not interested in leaving his stamp on the world; he is not seeking to be remembered by generations to come as a saint who made efforts to save his disabled son. He probably will not be acknowledged for his desperate struggle to care for his son, or even remembered at all. Mendel is also not interested in trying to cure his own sick and dying body or in spending his last days in joyful activities (e.g., spending money on lavish indulgences) that may allegedly compensate him for his miserable life. He is a man on a mission and the mission is a moral one: taking care of his disabled child, who is going to be left alone in the world.

After he finally gains the money, he needs to buy the train ticket and after finally reaching the train station with his son, death in the form of Ginzburg blocks their way. This is a moment of despair. Despite his odyssey and enormous efforts, Mendel seems to miss the train, literally and metaphorically. However, even at this point, Mendel's only concern is his son. "For myself," he begs, "I don't ask a thing. But what will happen to my boy?" The angel of death, who now appears in the form of a ticket collector, refuses to show any mercy or empathy, as expected from his well-known reputation. Given this reputation, most people would probably have given up. However, Mendel instead has a surprising fight response: he lunges at Ginzburg's throat and starts choking him while asking, "don't you understand what it means human?" At this point, when the old man is struggling with the devil himself, something interesting happens, as, when clinging to Ginzburg in agony, Mendel sees reflected in the ticket collector's eyes (i.e., death's eyes) the depth of his own terror.

Ginzburg, staring at himself in Mendel's eyes, sees mirrored in them the extent of his own awful wrath. He beholds a shimmering, starry, blinding light that produces darkness. At this point, death himself gives up and allows the poor father to enter the train station and to send his disabled son to California. Caring has beaten death, a victory that is in line with our innermost wishes—wishes that find no place in the real world, where one seldom wins a direct struggle with the angel of death. The trick, as Malamud teaches us, is to look directly in the eyes of death. The meaning of this mutual gaze, Mendel and Ginzburg's mutual gaze, will be clarified later in an interpretation of one of the Shakespeare's plays through the writings of Bakhtin. For now, let us proceed and move on from caring and trust to cooperation.

Bateson (1988) hypothesizes that *cooperation* is like parental care and has developed for similar reasons. Caring therefore precedes cooperation and is deeply associated with trust, as *trust is the prerequisite for caring*. Bateson also points to the benefits of trust in terms of cooperation and survival of both groups and individuals. Therefore, trust is an accompanying aspect of threat. While threat assessment is shared by many species, complex social species have developed cooperative means that emerge from basic nurturing and defensive parental patterns. In this context, how should we understand trust?

Some of the literature dealing with trust has for many years been inclined toward a rational choice perspective. For instance, Gambetta (1988, p. 127) writes,

> When we say we trust someone or that someone is trustworthy, we implicitly mean that the probability that he will perform an action that is beneficial or at least not detrimental to us is high enough for us to consider engaging in some form of cooperation with him.

As we can see, this economic approach includes some kind of risk assessment, which is a common denominator of both threat and trust management. However, this game-theoretic approach has been questioned for two main reasons. First, despite the widely held rational conceptualization of human beings, it has recently been argued that trust is not exclusively dependent on economic dynamics but also on social and emotional factors. While trust is influenced by social and emotional factors, the rational risk-assessment component cannot be totally dismissed; given the laboratory experiments of researchers in economic psychology, it should be qualified and refined. As will be presented later, our trust system is probably grounded in *two distinct neurological systems*, one dealing with a "rational" evaluation of uncertain situations and the other more emotionally oriented and grounded in our reward system.

The second point of consideration regarding the rational choice perspective on trust concerns the grounding of trust in our early experience as infants. It is doubtful whether an infant can make rational risk-assessment calculations that underlie the rational choice perspective on trust. In fact, there is no supporting evidence that infants can make such rational calculations. That is, from a *developmental* perspective, *trust is evident before any rational calculations can be made*. In this context, the full intentional meaning of "expectation" or "anticipation" should be theoretically and empirically clarified. It may be revised to adjust it to the cognitive-biological context. What does it mean that a newborn baby *expects* caring and that he trusts his mother to nurture and defend him? First, we should reject the rational economic approach with its reliance on individualistic and probabilistic terms. The idea that our minds behave like an actuary of an insurance company is probably wrong. The reasonable meaning of a "rational choice" in its animalistic context of trust is that a rational choice should not necessarily assume "intention" or conscious rational calculations on the *individual* level of analysis, and that we may shift the burden of rationality to evolutionary mechanisms that exist at the *species level of analysis*. This point can be explained through infants crying.

ON CRY AND TRUST

For the infant, crying involves an intensive expense of energy. It is a signal of stress but also an expression of fitness—that is, the infant who cries loudest is the most energetic and therefore may have the best chance of survival (Soltis, 2004). Therefore, the infant's "trust" does not have to be explained through an intentional, calculated, conscious, and economic mental act. It is the *hardwired anticipation of being nurtured, defended, and calmed* and the *signaling of stress* to attract the attention of the caring mother/father.

It is debated whether early infant crying is a behavioral state indicating discomfort or pain or a signal to attract the caring mother/father. Soltis (2004) provides a comprehensive discussion of early infant crying (up to 3 months) from an evolutionary perspective. He suggests that infant crying is a communicative signal conveying the infant's distress. However, adopting the idea of parent–child conflict, he also makes the interesting argument that there is overwhelming cross-cultural evidence suggesting that the reduction or withdrawal of optimal care when child-rearing circumstances are unfavorable is a prominent feature of human evolutionary history. He further argues that such an environment of uncertain parental care produces a strong selective pressure on the human infant that can influence the behavior of potential caregivers.

In this context, he also suggests that chronically and severely abnormal infant crying signals an infant's poor health condition, which has been the cause of neglect, infanticide, or abuse much more common in human history that we might imagine. In other words, the cry is a signal inviting caring but it may also signal the infant's poor health and may under certain conditions lead to a negative response from parents. *Infant crying is therefore a sign rather than a signal as it may be interpreted in diametrically opposed senses*, one leading to life-saving behavior (e.g., caring) while the other to death (e.g., infanticide). It means that *the infant's most basic trust in the world is imbued with ambivalence* as his crying might lead to contrary results. *Trust is therefore always engendered with threat*. This important conclusion gives no place to oversimplistic and mechanistic conceptions of personality, as the attempt to ground personality in basic biological processes is found to be "semiotic" through and through. There is no way of avoiding the process of interpreting a sign, even when studying a basic and nonreflective behavior such as baby's cry. This is the reason why trust in others is always imbued with the threat of treason as our anticipation of caring, when communicated to others, might be used against us. As expressed by Lord Hastings in Shakespeare *Richard III* Act 3,

> O momentary grace of mortal men,
> Which we more hunt for than the grace of God!
> Who builds his hopes in air of your good looks,
> Lives like a drunken sailor on a mast,
> Ready, with every nod, to tumble down
> Into the fatal bowels of the deep.

Do not trust human beings, advises Shakespeare in many of his plays. However, trust is inevitable and therefore human beings must find ways of living with the tension between trust and distrust in a threatening environment. This is an excellent place for a short break to discuss *trust violation* and what con artists can teach us about trust.

STREET CONS KNOW ABOUT TRUST

If you are interested in learning about trust, go and ask those who make their living by manipulating trust, such as street cons. In the context of computer security, a computer scientist joined two confidence tricksters to analyze and replicate scams that appeared in the TV series *The Real Hustle*. In this show, the expert "tricksters" identified the most common scams in Britain and showed how they work on innocent people while filming the deception with hidden cameras. The most significant scams were documented and discussed in a paper by Stajano and Wilson (2011) and we will discuss some of them to better understand the psychology of trust, specifically in the context of trust violation.

The first type of scam, titled "Monte," involves a procedure often witnessed as part of entertainment shows. The con uses three cards, shifting their locations on a table while they are facedown. Participants attempt to identify the location of a certain card and win something if they are successful. The scam is very simple. Several demo runs are performed in which the victim observes other people, cooperating with the con, winning; the victim may also himself win. Having been seduced into the game, he finally loses his money. The logic of his deception is described by Stajano and Wilson (2011, p. 5) as "nothing is what it seems" and as a failure to understand that this is *not* a fair game. This logic is highly relevant to reading some of Shakespeare's plays, as "nothing is what it seems" not only concerns visual illusions but also the illusion of trust. Trust, whether in the context of street cons using Monte or in social interactions, involves a kind of childish naiveté in believing that "what you see is what you get" and that if you are invited to take a part in a (social) game, it will be a fair game where you have a chance of winning. Trusting other people is biased toward such expectations as babies do not have an alternative. They must trust their caregivers. Understanding the potentially treacherous nature of trust is possible through a developmental process in which we (should) learn the complexity of trust management. A healthy, mature sense of trust cannot involve childish naivety in which one blindly believes in what one is told.

Yiddish, the dialect spoken by European Jews in the past, has a nice phrase for describing a deceptive situation. This phrase may be translated as, "He has been fed with noodles." This phrase alludes to the oral-dependent position of someone who has been fed with "lies." Noodles are a soft kind of food and the victim of the con is described as an oral-dependent baby who cannot control or even resist what he is being fed. We trust those who feed us even if they feed us with *lokshens* (the Yiddish term for noodles). Now let us return to our hustlers.

The aforementioned paper describes several main principles used by hustlers. The first is the *distraction principle*, which refers to being one step ahead of the victim and *paralyzing his threat-identification processes*. The victim is "directed away from the scam and towards that which they desire" (Stajano & Wilson, p. 10). Anesthetizing the rational and critical aspect of our trust system seems to be a leading principle of cons. No risk assessment is used when one is deceived. Therefore, a crucial component of deception is somehow anesthetizing our critical rational ability and bringing us into the situation of a dependent baby who is being fed *lokshens*. The "social compliance principle" exploits people's tendency to *obey authority* and it is a principle that is deeply related to social status. Following an authority and the threat to social status are deeply connected. It is therefore not surprising to find that institutes and people who are organized around the idea of rank are those most susceptible to deception using the aforementioned principle. For our intelligence agent, entering a military base in the United States while disguised may, paradoxically, be simpler than entering a bistro held by the mafia in Naples. He just has to appear dressed in uniform with the insignia of a highly ranked officer to back up his deception, in case someone checks who is the guest who has suddenly popped up in the base.

The third principle, the "herd principle," suggests that "even suspicious marks will let their guard down when everyone next to them appears to share the same risks. Safety in numbers? Not if they're all conspiring against you" (Stajano & Wilson, p. 13). The "need and greed principle" states that "your needs and desires make you vulnerable. Once hustlers know what you really want, they can easily manipulate you" (Stajano & Wilson, p. 13).

We can see that the manipulation of trust involves both cognitive and social aspects that aim to remove our basic suspicions by addressing two main sources of threat: the threat to social status and the threat of "violence," expressed as risking our money, our "bread" (to use a slang word for money). Trust therefore deeply leans on social and cognitive aspects alike. Following the discussion so far, we may gain another layer of understanding of human personality. We may hypothesize, for instance, that a person with what is described as a "dependent personality" is someone whose trust system is infantile, who sees what he wants to see, and who clings onto others while being ready to pay them for a "game" that in many cases is exploitation. The reason that such a dependent personality is ready to fool himself is that its biggest threat is the one of *separation*, which might leave him helpless, like a neglected baby. The threat to the dependent personality is the threat of annihilation posed by separation and the nonresponse to communicated trust signs. The ultimate response of the dependent personality is flight—a flight into metaphorical unity with another person, into the metaphorical *holding* and embracing of a protecting other.

Are you familiar with the beautiful 1971 song by Bill Withers "Ain't No Sunshine"? This song has been covered by various singers from Barry White to Joe Cocker. The main theme is that there is no sunshine *when one's lover is gone*. Poor old Bill feels that the separation from his lover is such a catastrophic event that the sun, the ultimate source of light and life, is gone, and that the world has turned into a dark and dead place. I believe that this song should be adopted as the official anthem of the society of people suffering from dependent personality disorder, if there were such a society. One person who would be likely to join the society is Desdemona from Shakespeare's *Othello*. Her overly naive and clingy approach to her murderous husband positions her as a potential candidate to be the honorary president of such a society. And guess what kind of food should be served at the meeting of this society? You are correct: *lokshens*!

Here we may produce another hypothesis. The affective neuroscience approach proposes the concept of "seeking" (Davis & Panksepp, 2011), which is described as an appetitive motivation system that involves a goal-directed behavior, feeling curious, feeling like exploring, striving for solutions to problems and puzzles, positively anticipating new experiences, and a sense of being able to accomplish almost anything. Seeking may be traced back to infants' basic threat- and trust-management processes. A person characterized by a comparatively high level of seeking may be a person whose caring needs have been satisfied to a level that reduces the risk he attributes to potential threats. In other words, as "trust" is associated with risk/threat assessment in cooperative situations, and as we reduce trust to the anticipation of caring, an infant whose needs are satisfied and whose stress signals are addressed by nurturing (good enough) parents may learn that

1. the risk associated with a threat is low, that
2. through his neurological positive reward system he has some control over the environment (e.g., there is an association between a sign of crying and nurturing), and therefore
3. may feel more confident in investigating his environment and being playful.

This is precisely the context in which the secure personality is formed, according to the theory of attachment insightfully proposed by Bowlby. Therefore, seeking, which is considered one of the basic dimensions of personality proposed by the affective neuroscience approach, may actually be the result of threat- and trust-management processes. Another possible hypothesis is that the system of "playfulness"—proposed by the affective neuroscience approach to involve joy, social gaming, laughter, and humor—may also be the direct result of trust management. Playfulness is a result of the trust that accompanies good-enough caring and of confidence in "seeking" in the environment. This hypothesis is supported by the fact that a lack of playing skills among children is indicative of previous inadequate interactions with caregivers or other pathologies. In addition, playing has been described in the seminal work of Winnicott as inquiring or seeking a "potential space," an idea that also supports the aforementioned hypothesis.

In sum, we can see how a "groundist" approach to trust management is applicable to both human and some nonhuman organisms by reducing trust management to basic patterns of caring and signaling. We are born to anticipate caring as otherwise signals inviting it would not be transmitted. The crying baby would not attract his mother's attention unless there was an anticipation of the ability to communicate that he is hungry, suffering, or simply asking for a warm hug. Trust is deeply associated with caring and this association underlies recurring themes in Western culture. One such a theme is home seeking what the Greeks called "*Nostos*." The word "nostalgia," which means "longing for the past," is grounded in *nostos*. The *Odyssey*, attributed to Homer, is a text where the motivating force of the hero is to return back home. His *hope* is nurtured by the anticipation that his loving wife will wait for him, and of course will not cheat on him with other men. Trust, anticipation, and hope are therefore deeply linked.

TRUST VIOLATION

The theoretical perspective presented so far may help us to understand why the violation of trust results in a breach that is very hard to recover from. A cheated husband will probably find it difficult to forgive his wife, and a neglected child will probably develops mental disturbances, as extensively documented in the psychological literature. While the violation of *threat expectation* does not have negative results, the violation of *trust expectation* is asymmetrically loaded with negative affect and high arousal.

In this context, the difficulty of recovering trust may be explained as follows. Given a hardwired anticipation of caring, the *only* early "defense mechanism" given to the helpless human mammal is the signal of crying. That is, the most basic form of trust in the world involves *anticipation* and asymmetrical *communication*, similar to a message in a bottle waiting to be found. In other words, the infant is hardwired to risk his energy resources in crying by unintentionally and unconsciously anticipating that the sign will be positively responded to by a caregiver. When these two components of trust—*anticipation* and *communication*—fail to function, the most basic sense of trust is shaken, with implications that cannot be easily recovered. If one cannot trust the world, the world turns into an *incomprehensible and threatening chaos*.

As we grow up, we learn the complexity involved in trust. Trust is composed of both rational and "irrational" aspects. We may emotionally trust a person given certain trust cues, such as facial expressions, but cues of trust may be "refuted" given a negative experience with the person or given *a priori* knowledge about his trustworthiness. A smiling face is not necessarily an indication that a person can be trusted. This conclusion holds for trust as well as for the recovery of trust after a breach.

It has been argued (Schilke, Reiman & Cook, 2013, p. 15236) that "greater relationship experience before a trust breach fosters trust recovery." In other words, a rational form of assessment involving a previous experience has an influence on trust recovery. Moreover, using neuroimaging methodology, these researchers suggest that the length of the relationship before a trust breach is positively correlated with trust recovery. This conclusion, which draws on laboratory experiments, should be qualified as it contradicts our basic experience in the world. For instance, the above argument suggests that a man with a 10-year-long marital relationship with his spouse will find it easier to forgive his cheating wife than a man with a one-month period of involvement with his new girlfriend will. My own theorization generates a diametrically opposed hypothesis. The longer the relationship history and the more rewarded are the anticipation/communication and caring interactions, the more difficult it will be to recover a breach in trust. This hypothesis is in line with the findings (Fouragnan et al., 2013, p. 3602) that

> When no prior information on transaction partners is available, the brain's reward circuitry is involved in learning about their type (i.e., their level of trustworthiness), based on the outcomes of previous trust-based interactions.

Indeed, reward-related brain regions have been found to respond positively to trustworthiness and negatively to violations of trust. In other words, brain reward circuits underlying what is called "reinforcement learning" are involved in strengthening the anticipation of trust given positive learning and vice versa. Fouragnan et al. (2013) suggest that another factor may be taken into consideration, which is prior experience provided by a third party. That is, our trust in others may be influenced by not only first-hand rewarding or nonrewarding interactions with this person as guided by hardwired mechanisms but also information provided by others. We will see later when reading Shakespeare's plays that this source of information is sometimes used to manipulate others. For example, Iago—the ultimate villain of Othello—is a third party who "informs" Othello about his "cheating" wife Desdemona.

Moreover, Fouragnan et al. (2013) found that prior information was associated with brain activity in a region that was found to be involved in *uncertainty resolution* in interactive contexts. When no priors were evident, the researchers measured increased activation in the caudate nucleus, which is involved in *reinforcement-based learning*. They summarize their findings by suggesting that the existence of prior expectations regarding the trustworthiness of a person has a powerful influence on the risk assessment and evaluation of a counterpart in a case of trust violation. Knowing that someone has a good reputation may therefore have a moderating influence on his assessment given a trust violation, as this breach is judged given the context, background knowledge, and possible attribution of the breach to extenuating circumstances. This is precisely what we will see in *Julius Caesar*, in which Brutus, the "honorable citizen," is "trusted" even after his involvement in the assassination of Caesar as his reputation is so strong that it cannot be refuted.

From an evolutionary developmental perspective, the infant's trust is firmly based on his *evolutionary priors* as he is born to anticipate caring parents. Therefore, a breach in basic trust, despite its detrimental consequences, may overshadow the lesson learned from more basic reward systems. An abusing mother is still evolutionarily primed to be conceived as a "good enough mother," to use Winnicott's famous term. In other words, despite the fact that abusing or neglecting parents activate a negative reward system, the priors of the evolutionary trust system cause the infant to anticipate caring parents, thus moderating the perception of the parents' negative behavior.

This hypothesis explains why young children are still attached to abusing parents and only at a later age—when more complex cortical regions may become fully activated—can critically evaluate their parents' wrongdoing and process the conflict they have experienced between trust anticipation and the abusing actions. Let us recall the paranoid personality and examine how it can be interpreted in light of the neurobiology of trust. The paranoid personality disorder, which is characterized by a conflict of trust, may be studied as manifesting a deep conflict between (1) the priors of trust and (2) the learned trust/distrust experience. In this context, the asymmetry of trust and distrust should be discussed.

ON THE ASYMMETRY OF TRUST AND DISTRUST

There is some evidence that distrust is not simply the absence of trust but qualitatively and neurologically different. For example, Long, Jiang, and Zhou (2012) measured the P300 brain signal, which has been shown to encode various aspects of feedback stimuli, including the magnitude of the reward. They found a significant effect following trust choices but a nonsignificant effect following distrust choices. Another indirect support for the neuropsychological difference between trust and distrust may come from *appetitive processing*. "Appetite for life," or what has been described in the literature as "appetitive processing" (Bradley, Codispoti, Cuthbert, & Lang, 2001), seems to be associated with the striatum (e.g., Delgado, 2007), the same locus in the brain that is associated with trust processing. Indeed, hope has been metaphorically described as bread, and therefore trust, hope, and appetite are closely related.

A depressed person who has no hope is someone who has no "appetite" for life. Depression is the ultimate psychological flight strategy and we can hypothesize that it is associated with a loss of trust and deactivation of "appetitive processing." Following the same line of reasoning, anorexia, at least from a psychological perspective, may be described as a loss of "appetitive processing," which is a depressive response and a failure to appropriately manage the trust and threat systems.

Along the same lines, it has been found (Choi, Padmala, Spechler, & Pessoa, 2014) that when reward and threat were jointly present, reward opposed the effect of threat and vice versa, confirming the "competition hypothesis," which suggests that the processing of reward and threat will trade off against each other. This finding suggests that *trust associated with reward* and *distrust associated with threat* are probably grounded in two different neural systems. In this context, Dimoka's (2010) study on the neurobiological aspects of trust has several interesting findings. It identifies potential neural correlates of trust and distrust, showing that trust is associated with the brain's *reward, prediction, and uncertainty areas*, while distrust is associated with the brain's *intense emotions and fear of loss areas* (Dimoka, 2010, p. 388). That is, while trust has both rational and emotional aspects, distrust is more inclined to the affective systems of fear and sadness (Davis & Panksepp, 2011), which are associated with abandonment and separation, a conclusion that is perfectly clear given the developmental aspect of distrust as being associated with abandonment and separation associated with caring others.

We may conclude by suggesting that threat, trust, and distrust involve different neural systems. Trust involves the expectation of care and is associated with uncertainty concerning whether such an expectation will be fulfilled and with a deeper uncertainty concerning whether such a communicated expectation will be abused. Distrust involves threat processing and the fear and sadness of separation. The following discussion aims to summarize and integrate the ideas presented with regard to threat- and trust-management processes.

DISCUSSION

In this part of the book, I have presented a theory of personality that is grounded in threat- and trust-management processes. Integrating theoretical and research findings, it seems that a cognitive-biological overview can unify the various approaches to personality and provide an integrative explanation for various personality types, given the complexities produced by the more abstract level provided by our cultural meaning-making systems. Personality is considered to be constituted by the threat and trust systems, where a distrust system holds a unique position between trust and threat and involves on one hand attraction to a stimulus and on the other hand threat and fear of the stimulus.

The threat and trust systems both involve *a priori* and more "rational" aspects of social information processing under uncertainty while at the same time more basic affective systems based on positive/negative reward experience. At this point, the explanation of the neuroticism personality dimension of the five-factor model through the threat–trust system is inevitable. Neuroticism is one of the most basic dimensions of the five-factor model as it involves an essentially negative approach to life and self. As argued by DeYoung and Gray (2009, p. 333; emphasis mine), various brain systems associated with reactions to *threat* and punishment have been linked to neuroticism, and neuroticism appears to reflect sensitivity to *threat* and the whole range of negative emotions and cognitions that accompany experiences of threat and punishment, including anxiety, depression, anger, irritation, self-consciousness, and vulnerability. Simply interpreted, being neurotic means (1) being highly sensitive to various threats and experiencing the various negative emotions associated with threat, and (2) a flight response in which the dominant response strategy involves psychological distancing from the threat, to the "inside." This is one case where the theory can provide us with a simple explanation of a personality dimension that has been intensively studied in psychology.

To understand how threat and trust are associated with the personality types discussed in the psychodynamic approach, we should recall that threat assessment involves not only the search for signals of threat and their attribution to a specific source (e.g., status threat) but also the ad hoc assessment of the threatening situation and the extent to which situational constraints may support one or more of the basic response types—flee, freeze, or fight—that among human beings may be abstracted to defense mechanisms such as avoidance.

In their comprehensive study of personality dimensions from a psychodynamic perspective, Westen et al. (2012) generate an empirically derived personality taxonomy in which personality types are organized according to two main clusters, or what they describe as "spectrums." The *internalizing spectrum* involves individuals who on the pathological aspect experience painful emotions, mainly depression and anxiety. They are emotionally inhibited and socially avoidant and tend to blame themselves for their suffering, therefore, turning their rage against themselves. This spectrum includes the following personality types: depressive, anxious–avoidant, dependent–victimized, and schizoid–schizotypal. These are neurotic personality prototypes that are mostly *threatened by status* and by the emotionally negative consequences of social rejection, and who assess the situation as unsolvable ("I can't deal with it") and therefore respond to it by fleeing (i.e., avoidance). They are therefore introverts who turn their rage against themselves and are therefore characterized by depression, which we have interpreted before as a lack of trust in caring others who may support them, plus a flight response. This hypothesis brings us to extraversion, which is another major factor discussed by the five-factor model of personality. DeYoung & Gray (2009, p. 331) suggest that several neuroimaging studies have found that brain activity at rest or in response to *positive or rewarding stimuli* is positively associated with extraversion.

Therefore, being an extravert is clearly associated with the trust system accompanied by "seeking" (Davis & Panksepp, 2011) and appetitive behavior. An extravert is simply someone who has a developed a trust system that is accompanied by appetitive processing, a positive fight response. The above-mentioned finding also explains why individuals characterized by Westen et al. (2012) on the pathological internalizing spectrum withdraw from social interactions. As they feel threatened by social rejection and as their reward and approach/appetitive behavior is limited, introverts do not turn "outside" to seek help and to cope with their anxiety; instead they withdraw and flee from the threatening interpersonal situation. Simply stated, introversion is running away from the threatening environment, and as such, it is a typical flight response.

In the Israel Defense Forces, soldiers are taught how to respond to a situation in which they are surprised by gunfire directed at them. The procedure, established a long time ago, counterintuitively directs soldiers first to respond by firing at the source of the threat and only then to seek a hiding place. The "psycho-logic" underlying this procedure is that a fight response is necessary to avoid falling into helplessness. The idea that one is in an inferior and life-threatening situation almost automatically results in despair. Getting out of despair is possible only by adopting a proactive approach, which is quite counterintuitive to the immediate urge to look for shelter. The psycho-logic underlying the procedure taught to the Israeli soldiers is grounded in the theory presented so far.

In contrast with introverts, individuals who are located on the pathologically opposite *externalizing spectrum* (i.e., antisocial–psychopathic personality, paranoid personality, and narcissistic personality) are characterized by anger and hostility and the projection of blame on others. Therefore, they are neurotic personalities who are threatened by attack, consider the situation as allowing only a fight response, and turn their fear and rage against others. As we can see, the theorization proposed in this book can straightforwardly explain the variety of personality traits, from those discussed in the five-factor model to those discussed by the psychodynamic literature. Here is another example. DeYoung and Gray (2009, p. 334) suggest that "conscientiousness," the five-factor model dimension characterized by a high level of organization, appears to reflect the tendency of an individual to maintain motivational stability, to make plans, and to carry those plans out in an organized and industrious manner. The conscientiousness factor is clearly associated with the obsessive personality, which Westen et al. (2012) describe as emotionally constricted, conflicted, and rigid. Conscientiousness is the five-factor model factor that is most associated with the *distrust* system, the fear of contagion, and the freeze response. We can therefore propose that the conscientiousness and obsessive dimensions of personality are tags describing the dynamics involved in facing a certain imaginary and abstract threat (i.e., contagion), and are associated with the operation of the distrust system and with abstracted or one might say "metaphorical" freeze responses and an uncontrolled desire to get control over the situation.

In sum, the delicate balance between the threat and trust systems—with their accompanying sources of threat identification, modules of risk and situation assessment, and associated affect and defensive responses—seems to provide a unifying framework for understanding human personality. While personality can be reduced to the unique combinations of the threat and trust systems' parameters, the most salient difference between human and non-human organisms is grounded in the higher abstraction level of the human beings and their ability to generate and process their representations of threat and trust. For example, abstracting the notion of the contagion threat, human beings may consider abstract ideas as a source of threat. Along the same lines, religious ideas, political ideologies, and so on may be considered by human beings through metaphorical reasoning as "poison." Therefore, personality, as a way of modeling interpersonal relations so as to manage anxiety and coping strategies, may be grounded in the threat and trust systems and in their unique parameters and the ad hoc decisions that stem from them. However, one should not ignore the differences between human and nonhuman organisms, which add complexity to the emerging personality structures. Here is the place where we should fully understand why the personality of human beings is on one hand fully reducible (i.e., grounded) to our more basic biological nature and, on the other hand, meaningless without taking into account culturally mediating schemes and the developmental processes that shape the way we use them. Further is in the next chapter.

Chapter Four

We Have Always Been Too Modern

How to Weave Together the Biological and Cultural Threads of Personality

The theory presented before suggests that our personality can be grounded in but not reduced to our cognitive–biological mechanisms. Following Luria and Vygotsky's seminal work and Voloshinov's semiotic psychology, I explain how the biological, developmental, and cultural threads are woven together to constitute real and complex personalities.

Previously, I proposed the idea that human personality can be grounded in cognitive-biological mechanisms of threat and trust management. This is not a simple reductionist move in which human personality can be *simply* understood by breaking it down into simpler components. Human personality is grounded in basic processes but cannot be reduced to them. The difference between "reductionism" and "groundism" is highly important and can be explained via an analogy that concerns our ability to abstract. Human beings are unique in their ability to use abstract language that is detached from any concrete context and experience. For instance, when describing a baby as "sweet," I do not mean that the baby has a sweet taste . . . unless I am a cannibal. We use the term "sweet" in an abstract sense and as a synonym for "friendly," "attractive," and so on. It is possible to argue that the abstract sense of "sweet" is *grounded* in our sensory experience of a pleasant sugary taste (Neuman, Cohen, & Assaf, 2015). However, the abstract meaning of "sweet" cannot simply be reduced to the sensory experience per se as in this case, a bee and a human being would have the same understanding of "sweet." Some additional theorization is needed to explain how the abstract meaning of a word such as "sweet" emerges from the basic experience of humans (Neuman et al., 2015). Along the same line of reasoning, the processes of threat and trust management—as described in the previous chapter—may be basic processes for understanding personality, but some additional ingredients are needed in order to understand the complexity of human personality, and these ingredients involve the semiotic social processes in which we are immersed.

The theoretical foundations for understanding the complexity of human personality can be found in a text that I consider to be one of the most important books ever written in psychology. The book is titled *Marxism and the Philosophy of Language* and it was written by Valentin Voloshinov in 1929 (Voloshinov, 1929/1986). Voloshinov's radical proposal, which struggles with both biological reductionism and its complementary "upward" form of reductionism—idealism—is that the "inner psyche" can be comprehended only as a semiotic phenomenon. Our first-person perspective, argues Voloshinov, is located on the border between the inner biological world and the outside social environment. It is a place of encounter where meaning is produced. Think, for example, about the experience of mourning. Losing a person to whom one is close is a psychological experience that is meaningful only when comprehended as our unique cognitive and emotional way of representing the reality of death, specifically the death of a significant person. Therefore, meaning always involves a *relation* and a relation represented through signs. Meaning is a relation as it is never the thing in itself but its *re-presentation*. The meaning of death cannot be found in death itself. The meaning of food cannot be found in the proteins, minerals, or vitamins that the food contains but in its meaning as a life-supporting source of energy. A baby's cry is meaningful only as it signals a need for care and because we understand that it signifies that need. Meaning is therefore always "about," and this "about" is constituted through a symbolic social system. Therefore, meaning is the expression of "a semiotic relationship between a particular piece of reality and another kind of reality that it stands for, represents, or depicts" (Voloshinov, 1929/1986, p. 28). Interpreting a verbal utterance as an insult is comprehensible only as a meaning-making activity that involves the representation of a certain sound pattern or visual gesture comprising negative emotionality and threat to status.

Human beings have acquired and developed a highly sophisticated form of meaning making, which is natural language, a system that develops toward higher levels of complexity. On the psychological level of analysis, this meaning-making system is expressed as *inner speech, a process in which we talk to ourselves.*[1] Our most significant form of meaning making thus involves the *internalized* counterpart of the verbal interactions and communicative patterns we experience with others, specifically with significant others. Indeed, there is evidence from neuroscience that inner speech activates brain areas that process language and that inner speech is the major platform for the emergence of consciousness (Morin, 2011). In this sense, our psychological understanding of human beings is deeply entangled with the social realm, where meaning is formed through interactions between subjects in a given context.

As language is always social (i.e., there is no "private language"), we must conclude that our inner experience reflects (but also refracts) processes of meaning making that exist at the *collective* or social level of analysis. The degree to which these cultural forms of meaning making are expressed in our minds is astounding. For instance, the idea of a god or gods is a recurring theme in the hallucinations of psychiatric patients. The famous case of Judge Schreber (1903/1988), who was intensively analyzed by Freud, is the only one case that illustrates this phenomenon. However, it has been found that, despite the fact that God is a recurrent theme in these hallucinations, God is surprisingly missing from the hallucinations of Jewish schizophrenic patients (Perez, 1977)! This is a unique finding explainable in terms of the highly abstract nature of God in Judaism. That is, despite the portrait of schizophrenia as deeply grounded in a biological disorder per se, the "inner experience" of schizophrenia is characterized by a variety of meaning-making processes mediated by the "sign community" (Voloshinov, 1929/1986) to which the patient belongs.

Several important clarifications should be considered with regard to the ideas presented so far. First, the idea of the human psyche as a "semiotic" phenomenon cannot and should not be confused with some postmodernist ideas about relativism. Voloshinov presents a structuralist perspective according to which patterns and regularities can be found in the human mind. His proposal is to look for these patterns in the way in which inner experience is mediated through the available semiotic systems via which meaning making is shaped.

A second point is that language is not discussed by Voloshinov as a kind of a Chomskyan abstract mathematical system. As Voloshinov explains, "The actual reality of language-speech is not the abstract system of linguistic forms, not the isolated monologic utterance, and not the psychophysiological act of implementation, but the social event of verbal interaction implemented in utterance or utterances" (Voloshinov, 1929/1986, p. 94). What is important for Voloshinov is the *pragmatics* of language—the way in which meaning is formed in context through the communication of individuals.

At this point, it is important to emphasize that the *social* aspect of language concerns the way meaning making is formed through the joint collective activity of individuals. In this sense, Voloshinov would have probably considered the sophisticated communication between the members of a bacteria colony as the expression of a social activity of meaning making. The social aspect therefore is not limited to ideological or political activities, but at the most basic level, it is about the collective activity of meaning making among members of a certain community.

In this context, it is important to distinguish between two different aspects of the utterance, which is the basic unit of communication: its *theme* and its *meaning*. Theme concerns the *particular* and *irreproducible* aspect of the utterance. For instance, the utterance "What time is it?" has a different meaning/answer each time it is asked. In contrast, the meaning of an utterance is reproducible in all instances of repetition—it is generally clear that when a person asks "What time is it?" he wishes to be told the hour. Meaning is therefore described by Voloshinov as a technical device for the implementation of the theme. The reason "any true understanding is dialogic in nature" (Voloshinov, 1929/1986, p. 102) is that understanding has to be resolved *in between* the particularity of the theme and the *generality* of the meaning. Take, for example, the process of word–sense disambiguation. Words in language are usually "polysemous," meaning that the same word form may be loaded with different senses in different contexts. This is a highly economic function of language as the same word can be used to express various senses. Slang words provide wonderful illustrations of the polysemy of language. The word "cat," to use my favorite example, may signify the feline creature but may be also used to signify a jazz player. To understand the meaning of a word or a sign in a specific context, one has to rely on various *contextual cues*, which are mostly available through social interactions. Now we better understand why meaning making is necessarily social as the need to resolve the tension between the abstract and concrete aspects of communication is satisfied only *in between subjects*. As the source of ambiguity is the need to economically communicate given the constraints of the general/particular, the solution is in the communication itself, as it is managed, negotiated, and formed in between subjects.

The bottom line is that, despite the biological roots of our minds and personalities and the biological roots that we share with other organisms, we have always been "modern" in the sense that the symbolic activities that form our inner experience have accompanied the more basic processes. In this context, understanding human personality *in vivo*—outside the laboratory and the abstract formulations of academic psychology—involves paying close attention to the way in which human personality is formed through the duality of "theme" and "meaning," through social processes that rely on the themes of threat and trust management, and by trying to gain insights through the close reading of literature, which provides us with a laboratory experiment that is reproducible (i.e., the novel can be read again and again) but unique at the same time (i.e., the plot presents a particular and irreproducible slice of human experience). *That is, literature is a medium that "plays" on the tension between theme and meaning, which is the tension that constitutes our meaning making.* With these complexities in mind, we can move forward to the reading of Shakespeare's plays. The reader should be aware that my reading is psychological and minimally draws on literary criticism, which has become highly psychological (specifically through Lacanian reading) but is of minor relevance to the particular aim of this book. Please relax in your seats while the play begins.

NOTE

1. This inner speech is an internalized form of communication and is applicable to sign language as well.

Part II

SHAKESPEARE FOR THE INTELLIGENCE AGENT

Chapter Five

Julius Caesar

On Trust and Reason

The first chapter of this part of the book analyzes Julius Caesar *and the personalities of the two main characters of the play: Caesar and Brutus. It focuses on how the personalities of Caesar the narcissist, who is threatened by status, and Brutus the overly moralist, who is threatened by the purity of Rome, are entwined in a plot of trust and treason. The chapter explains why people like Brutus, Trotsky, and Edward Snowden should always be suspected; explains why people are threatened by narcissists who strive for power; and imparts an important lesson concerning how real prisoners playing* Julius Caesar *can teach the imaginary character of Brutus and the readers of the play, an important lesson.*

WHENEVER THERE IS DOUBT . . .

Ronin is a 1998 action film (Mancuso, 1998) that presents several ex-special forces soldiers and intelligence agents who are hired to steal a mysterious suitcase. In one of the scenes located in Paris, after they have been saved from a deadly ambush, two of the characters, Vincent—played by Jean Reno—and Sam—played by Robert De Niro—are sitting in a car while silently smoking French cigarettes called Gitanes.

The reader may wonder why is it important to mention the cigarette brand that the two characters are smoking. The reason I mention it is that—in a book titled *Shakespeare for the Intelligence Agent*—close attention to minor details is a must, specifically if one understands that humans' threat-identification system should be attuned to minor cues.

The mainstream personality psychologist may consider such cues as secondary to a character's gross personality type. It is argued by some researchers that personality is to a large extent genetically determined and that it is

55

a hardwired pattern that determines our relations with the world. Given this theoretical stance, knowing who you are in terms of personality type is much more important than knowing what you smoke.

If we are interested in understanding real human beings rather than their academic abstractions, attention to the underlying dynamics and *minor cues* may be much more important than putting human beings into the boxes of general personality types. When trying to understand a person, the brand of cigarettes that he smokes may be an informative cue—probably not the only cue, but a potentially significant one. As you may recall, proactively seeking minor cues of threat characterizes many organisms and our reading of personality may also be inspired by this proactive approach to minor cues.

Personality types are names we use to describe emerging patterns of thoughts, emotion, and behavior, but inferring features of emotion, thoughts, and behavior from a personality type is a problematic move. For example, the term "paranoid" is used to describe someone who has a deep conflict with trust, as is specifically evident in high vigilance and suspiciousness. Adopting the perspective of Bayesian inference, we may ask, what is the probability of being paranoid given an extreme level of vigilance and suspiciousness? However, we may also ask the reverse question: What is the probability of being vigilant and suspicious given the title "paranoid?" Answering these two different questions is a tricky issue as, *by definition*, a paranoid is someone who presents high levels of vigilance and suspiciousness!

The difficulty is that what we conceive as a "personality type" is not a solid and monolithic entity that exists *independently* of its defining features but a category that is abstracted from certain observations. So what? Let me explain the problem through a concrete example. Let us assume you have a colleague by the name of Serpino. Serpino is highly suspicious and attributes malevolent intentions to others' thoughts and behavior. At dinner, you describe Serpino to your wife, who is a psychologist, and she immediately responds by saying, "Sure, Serpino is a clear case of a paranoid." Let us also assume that you have never heard the psychological term "paranoid" and ask your wife for an explanation. She explains that a paranoid personality is highly suspicious and attributes malevolent intentions to others. "Yes," you say, "but this is something that I already knew. What informative value if any exists in calling Serpino a 'paranoid'?" Your wife may further explain that this title describes a *pattern*. A pattern, she patiently explains, is actually a Gestalt, a set of interconnected elements that form a recognized structure.

The benefit in identifying a pattern is that, in seeing one part of it, one can expect to see the other parts as well. The human face is a kind of pattern. When you see your neighbor's forehead and eyes above your gardens' shared fence, you can expect him to have a nose and a mouth too. Describing Serpino as a paranoid is just a heuristic that may point to other aspects of his emotion, thoughts, or behavior that you may not have been aware of, for example, that Serpino has unjustified doubts about the loyalty and trustworthiness of his friends. You may respond first by questioning whether "personality" is a pattern similar to the face. Is it really a relatively stable configuration or a set of emotions, thoughts, and behavior that are adjusted and attuned to contextual constraints? Second, saying that someone who is highly suspicious in general is probably suspicious about the trustworthiness of his friends in particular is trivial. As someone who is not psychologically minded, you are concerned with more practical issues derived from diagnosing Serpino as paranoid. You may ask your wife, for instance, whether Serpino can be trusted as a colleague, whether he is likely to be cooperative in future ventures that you are planning, and so on. At this point, your wife may become impatient and the evening may slip into a "Who's afraid of Virginia Woolf" kind of interaction; it is better to open a new bottle of wine and enjoy a conversation about a less troubling issue.

I used the above example to challenge the commonsense wisdom of using the tags of personality types without critically considering their meaning. I have no objection to using personality types as a kind of nomenclature and I use these tags throughout the book, as they have become a part of our psychological lexicon. However, I would like to stress the fact that, in themselves, the personality tags are of negligible informative value and that, to understand patterns of emotion, thoughts, and behavior *in vivo*, it is more important to develop a sensitive approach to *dynamic patterns, their expression in petite cues, and their interpretation in real contexts*.

For example, I have an Israeli, albeit British-born, friend who responded with a snort of contempt upon hearing that I had bought a bottle of Jack Daniels. This response, which considered the consumption of American whiskey (more accurately "bourbon") as blasphemy, is an important diagnostic statement that, taken with other minor cues, may crystallize into a better understanding of my friend's "personality." If you are an American intelligence agent hesitating over whether to recruit my friend to work for the CIA, his British background and his allegedly innocent comment may be informative.

A confession. The aforementioned anecdote has nothing to do with my specific taste and personality; I am fond of Laphroaig, a heavenly Scotch produced on the Isle of Islay. The same friend converted my taste when he first introduced me to this nectar, the drink of the gods. As a footnote, let me just comment that the Greek word *nektar* is a compound meaning "overcoming" and "death." Indeed, a shot of excellent whiskey conveys the momentary illusion that "death shall have no dominion," to cite Dylan Thomas. We have drifted away, which is perfectly legitimate, and even obligatory, in a serious intellectual discussion. However, let us now return to the plot and the two characters, who are sitting in the car after having been saved from the ambush.

Sam is the one who realized, by noticing minor warning signals, that they were walking into a trap, and Vincent breaks the smoking silence by asking him how he knew it was an ambush. Sam replies by saying, "Whenever there is doubt, there is no doubt. That's the first thing they teach you." When asked who taught him this lesson, Sam avoids the answer, replying that he does not remember. However, we are easily led to the conclusion that his "teachers" were the instructors at the intelligence agency.

With a sufficient knowledge of Shakespeare, Vincent could have traced the "doubt–no doubt" wisdom to *Othello*, where the following sentence appears: "No! To be once in doubt is to be resolved." Both intelligence agents and some of Shakespeare's characters seem to share the same basic idea of trust and distrust and doubt and certainty. They are highly suspicious, not to say paranoid, in their approach to others.

In a situation where one's life depends on the delicate decisions that one has to make in real time, and in a context in which the price of making a wrong decision might be lethal, whenever there is a slight doubt about the trustworthiness of one's "business partners," the default is that there is no doubt; one's *heuristic* is to conclude with certainty that the others are *untrustworthy*. Given this rational context of decision-making, can we describe Sam's personality as paranoid? Is it possible to draw the conclusion that Sam's highly vigilant and suspicious behavior is indicative of his personality *regardless* of the specific context in which he operates? Do we have to define personality as stable patterns of thoughts, emotion, and behavior at the individual level of analysis? Or is it more accurate to look for the stability taking into account the context as well as the individual? As I have previously argued, "personality" is not an identity marker that we carry with us like our fingerprints. Personality is a term that describes the dynamic patterns through which we manage threat and trust and antagonism and cooperation—and varying contexts invite varying expressions of "personality."

It would have been unfortunate if Sam's behaviors were always vigilant and suspicious *regardless* of the context in which he operates. In this case, we would definitely consider Sam to be paranoid. In fact, a rule of thumb for defining a personality disorder is to look for *stable* patterns of thoughts, emotion, and behavior *regardless of the context*! For instance, the heroine in the movie is Deirdre, who is a young, attractive Irish woman and the arch-terrorist's right hand. Throughout the movie, it seems that there is sexual tension between Deirdre and Sam. We can imagine a situation where Sam and Deirdre are sitting in a Parisian bistro while the sexual tension between them reaches a climax. Finally, Deirdre approaches Sam and seductively whispers in his ear: "Shall we go to my place or to yours?" Sam may reply by saying,

"As there is doubt where to go, there is no doubt. Let's give the idea up. Good night." This imaginary scenario would portray Sam as a caricature of a paranoid, but one would seldom if ever meet such a grotesque personality in real-life situations. Sam is not a caricature of the paranoid personality. In the dangerous environment where he has to operate, the price of a false alarm is negligible compared to the price of committing the opposite error, which is missing the approaching threat, and therefore this is an environment that selects and socializes suspicious minds (i.e., "paranoids"). Again, this commonsense wisdom shifts the burden of personality from the person to the *person-in-context*. The idea is that—regardless of your "personality" or the way you manage threat and trust—in a dangerous situation, it is better to worry than to be sorry. However, in judging the situation, we use our predefined patterns of emotion, thought, and behavior. Some of these patterns are biologically determined; others evolve in us, developing from childhood to adulthood, and the rest are those we are provided by the culture in which we live.

Ronin presents extreme situations of threat and trust. In ordinary life, though, the boundaries between trust and distrust and between doubt and certainty are much more complex and confused even for fictive special agents like Sam. In real life, we have to struggle with doubt and continuously take the calculated risk that our trust in others will be abused even to the degree of treason. "Falling in love" is a metaphorical expression that beautifully grasps the excitement of being in love and the feeling of intimacy, openness, and trust in the loved one. At the same time, the idea of "falling" also points to the danger associated with establishing deep trust relationships with others. *The way we maintain this delicate balance is indicative of our "personality,"* or, more accurately, it is what personality is all about. It is not a mask—a static configuration imposed on us by our genes. *Personality is not only about transformation and conflict but also about maintenance and balance.* The way this balance is maintained in actual social contexts is indicative of the way personalities are constituted in practice. At this point, we may move to our first play—*Julius Caesar*—to understand how some of the play's major personalities are formed, and to try and gain some insights about personality.

BRUTUS, BRUTUS *LAMA SABACHTHANI*

Julius Caesar by William Shakespeare is a wonderful case for discussing human personality in the context of trust and treason. After all, in our collective mind, the most famous line of the play is the Latin phrase "Et tu, Brute?"—a phrase interpreted as the surprise and disappointment expressed by Caesar in realizing that Brutus—the honorable citizen, the son of his mistress, and according to some (improbable but psychologically intriguing) opinions, his biological son—is one of the traitors who are stabbing him to death.

From Shakespeare's original audience to the modern highbrow audience that is willing to struggle with the seventeenth-century English of Shakespeare, and via the popularization of the phrase "Et tu, Brute?" in contexts beyond the theater, Caesar's surprise and its presence in the collective memory of people through the ages is indicative of our deep interest in trust and treason, and can serve as a case study for understanding personalities.

The interest in trust and treason is a recurrent theme in Western culture. Caesar's surprise was not the first and will probably not be the last case in which the pain of treason and abandonment thrills us. When Jesus cried on the cross "Eloi, Eloi lama sabachthani," he was probably expressing the same pain of treason that generations of Christian scholars sought to explain. After all, why cry in pain and disappointment like an abandoned child when you are one-third of the omniscient deity that sent you to the human beings on a mission of redemption?

However, if we consider Jesus as a human being who trusts and hopes, a human being whose trust mechanism has been shaped through interaction with his caring parents, his pain and cry are perfectly comprehensible. In fact, merging the two texts—*Julius Caesar* and the New Testament—in our mind, we can even imagine Jesus crying "Et tu, Dieu?" expressing his surprise that God—the ultimate caring father—has betrayed him; but let us return to an earthly king, Julius Caesar.

To understand Caesar's personality, we have to understand his most famous line in the play: "Et tu, Brute?" Caesar's expressed surprise at the treason is trivial and nontrivial at the same time. We can imagine that, if he had been trained by the CIA, similar to Sam, Julius Caesar could have been taught to trust no one. In this case, he would have listened to his wife's good advice and avoided traveling to the senate on a day imbued with unnatural signs of warning. In some of Shakespeare's plays, such as *Macbeth*, the wife's advice is destructive. In Julius Caesar, the wives seem to be much more intelligent than their husbands.

While the scientific value of the unnatural signs guiding Calpurnia—Caesar's wife—can be qualified, her generally suspicious attitude could have saved Caesar's life (and his surprise at Brutus's treason). Whenever there is doubt, there is no doubt. In fact, Caesar's social environment invites suspicion, as the threat of assassination was a Damoclean sword hanging over the heads of all the Roman emperors. In this context, it seems rather surprising that Caesar behaves like a trusting person regardless of his context. This behavior cannot be simply explained by behavioral game theory unless we form a new approach to be titled "psychoanalytic game theory." There is no sense in putting the burden of proof on the context without taking into consideration that there is an individual operating within it.

Caesar's personality seems to be that of a soldier who has lost his sense of danger, at least publicly—a soldier who despises the idea that he might be conceived as a coward. He is a kind of *macho*, seeking to present his manhood and courage in public—and, as we have learned, courage is about a fight response. Caesar's personality is therefore a mask metamorphosis that results in a transition from a fearful human being, flesh and blood, into a fearless superman. At this point, we may identify an interesting difference between the soldier's and the intelligence agent's styles of thinking. While the soldier is following the ideal of the courageous lion, an image used by Caesar himself, the intelligence agent is more like a fox, showing extreme vigilance and suspicion in his behavior.

What would have happened if Caesar had been trained, like Sam, by the CIA and had gained the appropriate level of suspicion? In this case, and even if he could not prevent his assassination, the CIA-trained Caesar would have at least not been surprised by the conspiracy, and the shock he expressed in Shakespeare's play would have been replaced with something like, "What else could I have expected of you, assholes?" However, the dramatic tension created by Shakespeare, and our identification with Caesar's surprise at the treason, is possible only through our schemes of trust and its violation, and the way different people maintain this delicate balance *in vivo*.

To recall, we are born to trust, and as babies we send out our cries like a message in a bottle, hoping that they will be answered by our caregivers and later in life by those who care about us. Crying, for Caesar, may be a dangerous move as it may be interpreted as a sign of weakness. Now we understand that the persona of a fearless general is necessary to maintain his social status and avoid the threat of enemies. We have learned that trust is imbued with the danger and the threat of treason and we are well aware that there is no simple resolution to the trust issue. In contrast with Sam's conservative trust, we have to trust given the everlasting presence of threat and treason. This is precisely the context where Caesar operates.

Literature provides us with dramatic tension that refutes our wishful theoretical thinking that the world is simple and predictable. In our wishful-thinking world, our caregivers should always be trusted. The mother is always a perfect mother and if there are negative aspects to motherhood, they are projected onto the character of a "bad mother," a dynamic insightfully identified by the psychoanalyst Melanie Klein. Snow White's "bad mother" is the Evil Queen. Cinderella's mother is a loving mother but her stepmother is the dark side of the moon. In our wishful-thinking world, mom is always the good-enough mother as described by Winnicott, or its negative projection. However, in real life, those we trust most can be revealed as treacherous villains and vice versa, as illustrated in Shakespeare's plays.

We may conclude that reality is where the possible reigns and literature is the realm where, even though everything is possible, the characters are prisoners of the eternally repeated plot; thus, the actuality of certain possibilities crystallizes in our mind. This point is important to remember while reading a play, as literature's ability to crystallize the complexity and dynamic realm of possibilities may turn it into an important tool for understanding others and ourselves. Let us return to Caesar.

For a courageous army man like Caesar, trust, specifically in one's compatriots, is a necessary working assumption. As is well known to military psychologists, trust is the glue that maintains the coherence of the fighting squad. In this context of an ultimate trust-as-a-working-assumption, treason is experienced and considered as abandonment, the same abandonment experienced by Jesus when he uttered, "Eloi, Eloi lama sabachthani?" Jesus's cry, in the same way as Caesar's cry, is an indication of a violated expectation of trust. The soldier sent to the battle and the Messiah sent on a mission of redemption both expect some backup from their compatriots and commanders. They are personas socialized for "secure attachment," at least as their social working assumption. In contrast, for an intelligence agent like Sam, who interacts with double agents from both sides, trust is a dangerous working assumption. Given this introduction, we may delve deeper into the play.

ON GENTLEMEN AND THE THREAT TO STATUS

Julius Caesar opens with a clash between two social classes. Two tribunes—Flavius and Murellus—meet a cobbler and other "commoners" on their way to celebrate Caesar's victory over Pompey the Great. The noblemen seem to be disgusted by the cobbler's vulgar admiration of Caesar's victory over one of Rome's greatest sons. While he opposed Caesar, Pompey the Great was and remained one of the Rome's noble people, a distinguished member of *la familia.*

It seems that for the commoners, a victory is a victory, whereas for the noblemen, a victory is valuable as long as it follows a certain code of honor. To paraphrase Freud in an oversimplified manner, for the commoners, a cigar is just a cigar and a victory is just a victory that should be praised and celebrated. However, for the tribunes, as cultivated members of the high class, *a cigar is never just a cigar* and a victory is never a victory unless it is loaded with certain value.

As modern people, we may easily identify the tribunes' sophisticated moral stance and ridicule the *vulgos'* stance. However, from a critical perspective, the tribunes' moral approach should not impress us. The Roman *gentlemen* who impress us so much are actually echoing the etymological sense of *gentleman*. Originally, being *gentle* was not about being "kind" in the psychological personality sense of the term but about the appropriate behavior according to the moral norms of one's clan. The adjective "gentle" is grounded in the Latin *gentilis*, which means being of the same race, family, or clan. Being "gentle" originally meant being a member of "our" clan—someone whom we may trust as we know him. A person described as having a gentle personality is someone we may trust. However, the origin of this psychological observation is the social realm of trusting those we know—our family or clan members—in contrast with our distrust of foreigners. The psychological aspect of "gentle," therefore, involves a projection and abstraction that originated in the *social* realm in the same way as other personality dimensions that we have discussed in this book.

In sum, the personality dimension of "kindness" is not an individual characteristic that preceded the social realm. It is a personality dimension of trust that has been originated in the social arena and that through the evolution of our Western culture has been *internalized* and *individualized*. This position is clearly an antisolipsistic approach to personality analysis.

Our personality dimensions are (1) internalized forms of emotion, thought, and behavior; (2) grounded in our cognitive-biological heritage; (3) elaborated in the social realm; and (4) projected into our contemplating mind and back again the social realm, where they are continuously elaborated. This is a highly important point that should be remembered throughout the book.

According to the ancient idea of the gentleman, the Sicilian Mafia would have been considered by the noble Romans to be an impressive model of ethical behavior. After all, what is more impressive than defending your own clan while honorably slaughtering others? In other words, the tribunes' dissatisfaction with the commoners' enthusiasm is not necessarily a sign of superior morality but a social marker indicating their difference from the lower class.

The tribunes' dissatisfaction with Caesar's victory is shortly revealed as a dissatisfaction with Caesar himself. This dissatisfaction, in the same way as the tribunes' dissatisfaction with the commoners, is grounded in the *threat to status*. At the end of the scene, we find that the two noblemen are plotting against Caesar and explain their motives as follows:

> These growing feathers plucked from Caesar's wing
> Will make him fly an ordinary pitch,
> Who else would soar above the view of men
> And keep us all in servile fearfulness.

That is, the two noblemen plotting against Caesar are not only occupied by the urge to differentiate themselves from the commoners to establish their social status but also afraid that Caesar will subordinate them unless the feathers of this great eagle can be plucked to keep him from flying above and over their heads. Here we can learn something interesting about personality. Whenever there is a threat that a certain person will subordinate others, we may hypothesize that the threatening personality is a "narcissist." In contrast with the solitary, and one may even say "solipsistic," image of the narcissist falling in love with his own reflection, it seems that narcissism is primarily a concept grounded in our social interactions and conflict over status. Someone described as a narcissist is someone we suspect will inappropriately threaten our status by pretending to be better than they are. Hereafter, whenever I describe someone as a narcissist, I will use this "tag" to describe a social knot in which crossing threads of individual interactions are conflicted over social status and its negotiated legitimacy as an internalized dynamic. With this complexity in mind, we may progress in our reading of *Julius Caesar*.

Interestingly, the tribunes' intensive occupation with status is a personality-shaping fear that is grounded in and nurtured by cultural norms. The commoners can see Caesar's victory as a triumph as their status is not threatened. For them, the question "How low can you go?" (on the social ladder) is irrelevant. They are commoners and as long as they are given "bread and entertainment," their status is not threatened, at least not to the same degree as the tribunes. In contrast, the noble Romans, Flavius and Murellus, have their status threatened by a man who is metaphorically described as a kind of vulture flying "above" and "over" their heads. As a perceived threat to status is what characterizes the narcissistic personality, we should expect "narcissism" to be expressed in the higher class more than it is expressed in the lower class. The lesson is that, if we conceive personality in terms of threat- and trust-management processes, as proposed before, we should be very sensitive to the social and cultural context in which potential threats are framed. This is one clear benefit of adopting the theory I have proposed, as the theory can be applied to both the psychological and the social levels of analysis.

The personality of the noblemen, at least as expressed in the above dialogue, is very sensitive to the threat to status and betrays fear on that score. Status is an important aspect of one's persona, both as presented to others and as internalized by oneself. The way one manages threats to one's status is therefore an indication of one's personality, and personality is imbued with the social context, in which status and threat to status are conceived and managed.

The first lesson we learn from the play is, therefore, that the threat to status as built and managed in a given social system may be an important key to understanding the personalities involved. While the threat to status is evident in the tribunes' conversation, it is also the force that drives one of the main conspirators, as is evident in the next section. However, the current section invites a question concerning the extent to which the personalities that we study are grounded in cultural norms that exist beyond the individual unit of analysis. Is narcissism a personality trait of Flavius and Murellus, or is narcissism their personality as social characters (i.e., tribunes)? Can we and should we differentiate between the proportion of the cultural and the individual in their personality? My father, who studied as a child in an ultraorthodox Talmudic college—Yeshiva—remembered that the students were praised not for the answers they provided to certain questions but for the *questions* they produced to challenge their teachers. This may be a suitable attitude to adopt in the reading of this book. Instead of just giving answers, let us focus on the questions and challenges that emerge from a close reading of the text and let us also consider simple answers and explanations as a starting point rather than as a dead end for a discussion.

ON BRUTUS, THE MORALIST, AND THE WAY HE HAS BEEN SEDUCED

While the play is titled *Julius Caesar*, the real hero of the play is not Caesar, the great eagle, who is quite a boring character to tell the truth, but Brutus, the traitor. The villains in Shakespeare's play seem to be much more interesting than the other characters. Brutus's first (self-)introduction in the play is deeply psychological:

> I am not gamesome. I do lack some part
> Of that quick spirit that is in Antony.

This guy, as he presents himself, is not a "sport." He lacks a "quick spirit" and probably was not one of the high school "cool" guys. This self-presentation is a heuristic that invites certain expectations from others while at the same time it can be used by others to learn about the character of Brutus. One's personality is not necessarily a hidden marker but an explicit invitation for others to know what to expect from you. For example, let us assume that you are a high-school student in Miami, Florida and a new kid arrives in your class from Rome. In introducing himself, he says, "Good morning, my name is Brutus and I am not gamesome and I lack quick spirit." Given this self-disclosure and in an attempt to be friendly, you consider whether to invite young Brutus to the weekend pool party at your house, which is going to be accompanied by booze and dancing, or to ask your friend Mathew to invite the new guy to the weekly meeting of Palm Beach High School Philosophical Club. The next meeting is going to deal with

Heidegger's concept of *aletheia* and promises to be an exciting experience, at least for some. Given Brutus's self-introduction, most likely you would choose the second option. Therefore, personality is not only our pattern of managing threat and trust but also a pattern presented to others to invite certain forms of interaction.

Brutus is also a person who admits struggling with himself ("with himself at war") over an issue of which he is unaware, declaring that self-reflection is impossible ("for the eye sees not itself/But by reflection") and accepting his friend Cassius's proposal to serve as his looking glass. In other words, Brutus confesses that he is struggling with some inner unconscious conflicts that he cannot expose and politely invites the intervention of others. As we have learned, personalities are organized around conflicts and transformations. Therefore, we should be sensitive to what Brutus has to say about his "conflict." Presenting yourself as someone who is struggling over an unconscious issue is inviting others to inquire, even if only for the sake of curiosity, about that which is unspoken and cannot be spoken—to inquire what is the conflict and what is the hidden metamorphosis one seeks. Indeed, Cassius, who is Brutus's old friend, accepts the invitation and provides Brutus with the requested "reflection."

Cassius is an interesting character. He describes Caesar as a "sick girl" and later describes the Romans as governed by their "mothers' spirits" and "womanish" behavior. He seems to be a chauvinist. Cassius is also a vain person who is terrified by the imagined possibility of being enslaved by Caesar, to the degree that he threatens to commit suicide as a last resort. As there is no clear indication that Caesar has such a humiliating intention (to subordinate Cassius and others), Cassius's fear is clearly an imagined one. Attributing aggressive intentions to others is a defense mechanism described as "projection" and it characterizes the paranoid personality. But how do we know that the threat is imagined? Can we dismiss the possibility that Caesar has future plans that might hurt the good Roman Cassius? On whom should we put the burden of proof to clarify whether the threat is real, expected, or imagined?

Being subordinated is for Cassius being in the status of women, probably the thing he fears the most. As we can see, threat to status and fear of women go hand in hand. As women in Rome were subordinated to men, they signified a low social class. From Cassius's chauvinistic approach, we can learn an important lesson. Lacking empathy to others who are socially inferior and weak is grounded in our fear of losing status. We are afraid of the poor, the sick, and the hungry because imagining ourselves in their situation is a threatening thought that enacts the realization that life is based on shaky ground. Feeling empathy for others who are of a lower social status is grounded in our understanding that, in contrast with the Protestant capitalistic myth, our status does not reflect God's grace and the vicissitudes of life can throw us off the ladder at any point, regardless of God's (alleged) grace and mercy. While our talent and efforts are undeniably associated with our social status, we should remember that some people are born to contexts where they are practically doomed to a lower social status. A peasant who was born in ancient times could have been a talented person but changing his social status was probably impossible. Understanding those who are "inferior" is based on emotional *acceptance. Ipso facto,* we may conclude that those who lack empathy for people of lower social status and feel threatened by the idea of losing status are the people who have difficulty in accepting the uncertainty of real life and would like to control it, like Cassius. Caesar is indeed a potential threat, but an uncertain potential threat should not move the psychologically resilient person into declarations of suicide and plans of murder, as manifested by Cassius.

The reflection provided by Cassius to Brutus is actually a sophisticated psychological manipulation. It "reveals" to Brutus his inner conflict between his "love" for Caesar and the "general good," implying that Caesar should be removed from power (i.e., that Caesar should die). The dialogue between Brutus and Cassius should not be considered as a Socratic dialogue in which Cassius "delivers" the truth, to follow Socrates's metaphor, out of Brutus's inner self/womb. The dialogue is actually a psychological and discursive event in which Brutus *invites the reflection of what he already knows but refrains from publically admitting.*

In this context, Brutus, who lacks a "quick spirit," is incrementally exposed to us as a *rigid moralist* who prefers the abstract maxim of his superego to his true "love" of Caesar. While "superego" may be conceived as a pompous psychoanalytic noun, we have learned that it is actually a psychological term used to describe the way in which we *monitor* and *regulate* our thoughts, emotions, and behavior. In other words, the superego describes the way in which we *observe* ourselves (e.g., observe our inner speech) and *regulate* our thoughts, emotion, and behavior. In their turn, these activities turn to be a part of our personality. Old Freud, who is sometimes described as a hard-headed Cartesian who could not care less about what is going on outside our heads, suggested that the superego stems from our parents, who follow the conventions of society. As the way we observe and regulate ourselves is a part of our personality, we cannot avoid the conclusion that personality—while deeply grounded in our biological heritage—has a second and well-grounded foot in our social life. Some people who are described as having a rigid superego are living in this world with a list of recipes instructing them exactly how to behave. These people might punish themselves for the most negligible deviations from their plan. This way of thinking is also grounded in the ritualistic behavior evident among nonhuman organisms, a ritualistic behavior that aims to provide control over an uncertain and threatening situation. Brutus seems to be such a person.

In this context, it must be noted that Brutus is not a traitor of the greedy villain type. In contrast with Judas Iscariot who sold Jesus for money, Brutus is an honorable and highly respected citizen whose "good" motives after the assassination are not questioned even by his enemies.

In other words, because Brutus is a person who follows the (rigid) moral norms of his superego, he is highly appreciated by his friends and enemies, who—like other cultivated individuals—feel deep respect for those who prefer abstract moral norms to particular and "animalistic" urges. This is why it is difficult to hate Brutus, and Shakespeare's dramatic tension involves a psychological quandary regarding the deep psychological motives behind the treason performed by such an excellent and admired citizen—Brutus.

I believe that, interestingly and paradoxically, in his presentation of Brutus, Shakespeare points to the danger of the overmoralist personality and its potentially treacherous character. Why is it a paradoxical move? Because as morality is greatly appreciated, specifically in terms of high-class codes of honor, we might be inclined to believe that we can trust those who declare their ultimate commitment to Lady Justice, or in her Latin name Iustitia, the goddess of justice.

Here again is a point where personality is immersed with culture. The overmoralistic personality of Brutus is possible only in cultures where moral norms have gained a sacred status. While some psychologists would like us to believe that personality is universal, ahistoric, and decontextualized, it is difficult to imagine observing Brutus's "anal" personality among members of a group of hunter-gatherers thousands of years before abstract ideas of ethical norms gained their sacred status. In other words, Brutus's anal, overly moralistic, obsessive personality is deeply grounded in a culture where the abstract norms of ethics have gained a sacred status. Shakespeare is well aware that the most painful treason can emerge from those we trust most, and, surprisingly, from those who are least to be suspected of treason—the ultimate moralists.

This wisdom must have skipped the mind of Edward Snowden's supervisors. Snowden, whose treason was a serious blow to the US National Security Agency (NSA), was not a liberal activist who had been recruited to the NSA by mistake but someone who has been described by his colleagues as "more popish than the Pope." When I looked at some of Snowden's letters through novel tools I have developed for personality analysis, a clear "anal" dimension of personality surfaced. In his act of treason, as conceived by the government, Snowden, more popish than the Pope, the "teacher's pet" in the NSA, unsurprisingly followed the simple logic of his personality. People like Snowden and Brutus zealously follow the general and morally rigid norms of Lady Justice. They can be the best and most loyal members of an organization, but, at the moment they suspect their organization or colleagues of betraying these abstract ideals, they immediately become the organization's most bitter enemies. This "logic of converts" is well known, even if not at the conscious level of analysis, to revolutionary movements that, after taking power and removing their opponents, are quick to turn against their most cherished and ideological members.

For example, the famous Jewish Marxist leader and theorist, Leon Trotsky, born as Lev Davidovich Bronshtein, was expelled from the party, deported from Russia, and finally murdered in Mexico after opposing Stalin's power and bureaucracy. Murdering one of the revolution's most cherished sons was not only Stalin's personal whim but also a psychologically justified move of removing a dogmatic believer from the stage.[1] While I am not sure whether Stalin, a murderous paranoid, read and internalized the logic of Shakespeare's *Julius Caesar*, he definitely and deeply comprehended the psycho-logic of the dogmatic believers and zealous converts, and the threat they posed to the organization regardless of their enormous contribution to the revolution. Interestingly, it seems that Trotsky was a total failure in establishing personal relationships, and—while a charismatic orator and a leader in a time of crisis—he was unable to gain the affection and trust of people. In this psychological sense, Trotsky could not have been a serious threat to Stalin's regime. However, Stalin, for his own psychological reasons, demonized the power of Trotsky and strived to remove him from the stage. Paradoxically, those whom you can trust most are those who have the highest potential for lethal treason. Do not be impressed by the overmoralists, despite their charm.

Taking advice from Stalin, Caesar could have saved his own life by, paradoxically, suspecting those whose loyalty should never be questioned. Tragically, Caesar is blind to the danger of the overmoralist as his own personality prevents him from taking such a harsh step as questioning the loyalty of one who is more popish than the Pope.

ON THE COUCH: CASSIUS, THE PSYCHOANALYST, MEETS BRUTUS, THE PATIENT

While at this point Caesar seems to be blind to Brutus's dangerous personality, Brutus's personality is well understood by Cassius, who plays on Brutus's code of honor to seduce him to join the group of conspirators. Cassius's first psychological encounter with Brutus (Act 1 Scene 2) is in the form of evoking feelings of guilt. Cassius scolds Brutus for not showing love to his old friend (i.e., Cassius) who loves him so much. Brutus as an overmoralist personality hurries to apologize by putting the blame on himself, as expected, attributing his behavior to inner conflict—"conceptions only proper to myself." "Guilt" has its origin in words meaning "sin" or "crime." Guilt is, therefore, a psychological feeling of conducting a crime against the superego. Brutus feels guilty because any challenge to his rigid superego is conceived as a crime. Our Mr Perfect cannot stand the idea that he has done wrong. Cassius then creates a shift in the flow of discourse by asking a question that seems to move the subject to another topic:

Can you see your face?

Brutus negatively replies,

for the eye sees not itself
But by reflection.

Cassius is already prepared to provide Brutus with a reflection of his "worthiness" by the "best respect in Rome," those who speak highly of Brutus but wish that "noble Brutus had his eyes." At this point, Brutus suspects that he has been misled into "danger" and that Cassius is asking him to seek in himself "For something which is not in me." How does he know that this allegedly innocent conversation is leading him to "danger" and that Cassius is leading to some hidden thoughts that Brutus firmly denies? Cassius is willing to expose the "unconscious" of Brutus's mind: "That of yourself which you yet know not." This is a striking pre-Freudian use of the unconscious as a discursive move, similar to the way deeply elaborated by Michael Billig in his *Freudian Repression* (1999).

Cassius and Brutus share the same hidden motive—to remove Caesar from power. By attributing the murderous deed to Brutus's inner thoughts, Cassius is removing from himself the burden of guilt; it is Brutus who thought about the deed while Cassius the "psychoanalyst" served only as his looking glass. On the other hand, by giving Cassius permission to excavate and interpret his inner thoughts, Brutus can always deny his responsibility for the conspiracy as it originates in Cassius's interpretation, which can be denied and rejected if necessary. Like a patient participating in a psychotherapeutic session, Brutus can deny Cassius's act of mirroring. However, as in an act of tacitly agreed sexual seduction or flirting, both Brutus and Cassius share a deep understanding of what they are about to do.

When he hears the commoners' shouts and Brutus's confession that he fears that the people will choose Caesar for their king, Cassius lets the cat out of the bag:

Then must I think you would not have it so.

Brutus, however, is still struggling with his conflicts as he declares his "love" for Caesar. He is afraid, of course, that his love for Caesar will be misunderstood as a *barrier* to taking part in the conspiracy, and signals to Cassius that if he is asking him to do something for the "general good," this is perfectly legitimate, as

> I love
> The name of honor more than I fear death.

This is a point where the common ground for the conspiracy is established by Cassius, who declares "honor is the subject of my story." Cassius is the one who initiates the conspiracy but he well knows that his conspiracy will find fertile soil in Brutus by adhering to the overmoralist personality's code of honor. Brutus himself is not an innocent victim of brainwashing. Like an agent to be recruited against his country by a foreign intelligence agency, he is psychologically ready to betray Caesar and needs only a trigger.

The exchange that takes place between Cassius and Brutus involves the delicate and step-by-step process of establishing trust, a process orchestrated by Cassius's sensitive adherence to Brutus's personality. The step-by-step process of establishing trust aims to keep both individuals safe from a hasty self-disclosure that might mistakenly expose one of them as a conspirator while the other one is actually a supporter of Caesar. The process of establishing trust is therefore incremental and involves a high level of ambivalence, which may be used as an exit point whenever one of the interlocutors feels in danger and asks to withdraw from the process. Even Brutus, the overmoralist personality, is not ready to present himself as a potential assassin. While personality is sometimes portrayed as a static mask, we can learn from the interaction between Brutus and Cassius that it is actually a *dynamic* process that characterizes our interactions with others and with ourselves. Brutus's "anal" personality is not only uncovered but also built through his interaction with Cassius.

The second important aspect of the dialogue between Cassius and Brutus is the sensitivity to Brutus's personality so insightfully managed by Cassius. Although Cassius is quite negative about Caesar, describing him as a "sick girl" and flattering Brutus's sense of ego and importance, he keeps on track by declaring that "honor" is the subject of the story and by adhering to Brutus's loyalty to the "great good."

Brutus is not a person to be seduced through material goods or by appeal to his self-importance. Any attempt to recruit Brutus in a way orthogonal to his personality would have led to a total rejection of Cassius's kind proposal, but Cassius realizes that his "weak words" have sparked a fire in Brutus. "Weak words" is an interesting phrase. In his beautiful poem "So That You Will Hear Me," Pablo Neruda says to his lover that in order that she will hear him his words must "sometimes grow thin" (Neruda, 1969). To be heard, words should paradoxically "grow thin." In fact and as insightfully realized by Milton Erickson in his approach to hypnosis, only *thin or weak words* can strike a fire. The reason is that "strong words" might expose the hidden intentions of the person and evoke a counterresponse. Neruda's lover may be threatened by his passion and Brutus could have considered a direct approach to join the conspiracy as vulgar. Approaching Brutus directly by using "strong words," Cassius could have said,

> Listen Brutus, my man, I know that you are an obsessive–compulsive personality who can't bear the idea of someone violating your hard-headed idea of justice. As Caesar, who cried to me like a pussy to save him from drowning in a roaring river, is on his way to contaminate the purity of your sacred Rome, let's kick the living shit out of him.

This direct approach would probably have failed. Personalities are about hidden conflicts orchestrated in social interactions through "weak words," and when these conflicts are exposed, they lose their power, like a magic trick shamefully exposed by the audience. Personalities can exist as long as there is a shared consensus to let them work unconsciously or silently so that they can be negotiated in between individuals. The next section illustrates this dynamic by explaining how seduction is possible when flattering the narcissistic personality.

ON SEDUCTION, ELEPHANTS, AND HUMAN BEINGS

At the end of Act 1 Scene 2, Brutus is leaving the stage, and Cassius perfectly exposes his psychological manipulation of Brutus by saying to himself:

> Thy [Brutus's] honorable mettle [shape] may be wrought [bent]
> From that it is disposed. . . .
> For who so firm that cannot be seduced?

Indeed, the lesson we should learn is that probably most of us are not "so firm" and can be seduced, like Brutus the honorable citizen. Our trust and willingness to cooperate can be abused when the right chord of our personality is hit. Cassius is not the only seductive person in the play. When the conspirators gather and consider how to attract Caesar into their trap,

Decius volunteers to persuade Caesar to come. His approach is allegedly less complicated, as

> That unicorns may be betrayed with trees,
> And bears with glasses, elephants with holes,
> Lions with toils, and men with flatterers.

Decius explains to us the simple logic of hunting animals and humans alike. Unicorns may be trapped when their horn is entangled in a tree. Bears are misled by mirrors that probably dazzle the creatures with their own reflection. Elephants are directed to trenches covered with branches. Lions are caught with toils (nets such as those used by gladiators), and human beings, how simple, with flattery.

While Brutus is seduced to join the conspirators through a careful manipulation of his overmoralistic "anal" character, Caesar is brought to his trap through simple flattery, adhering to his narcissistic personality. Through Decius, his fictive character, we learn that Shakespeare does not think highly of human nature in general and of Caesar in particular.

Humans can easily be bought by flattery. In this sense, they are like the dazzled bears. However, while the bear is surprised by his image reflected from the looking glass, the human being—like the mythological character of Narcissus—is amazed by the grandiose self-image reflected to him from the flattering words. *Ipso facto*, we may conclude that humans have a basic dislike of criticism that diminishes their positive sense of self. The lesson we may learn from Shakespeare, and deliver to our intelligence agent, is never to send a judgmental and critical person on missions that involve some kind of persuasion or gaining trust. However, things are much more complicated. As flattery is an obvious trick, it can be expected and lose its efficacy. Indeed, Decius recognizes that flattery can be easily exposed:

> But when I tell him he hates flatterers,
> He says he does, being then most flattered.

Decius, as an expert flatterer, is expecting the most obvious counterresponse to flattery: You (the flatterer) do not consider me highly; you just wish to influence my mind! The flatterer who expects such a response can preempt it by praising the narcissistic persona for being *immune* to flattery. This is a move in which we compliment the narcissist for his grandiose self-sufficient personality, which can withstand what humans, like unicorns, are "betrayed with." In other words, immunity to flattery cannot be gained by pretending to be above the human, as all of us, according to Shakespeare, are easily "betrayed" by flattery.

Paradoxically, by having their susceptibility to flattery denied, human beings (and specifically narcissistic personalities like Caesar's) become prone to flattery and seduction. In fact, what we describe as a narcissistic personality may actually be described as a person who is highly susceptible to flattery. As this person is highly sensitive to his positive image and status among the members of his social group, he may be strongly inclined to be motivated to certain actions by those who reinforce his positive image in their allegedly objective mirror glass. "Mirror, mirror on the wall . . ."

Trust can be gained by flattery, which adheres to one of our most basic needs—to be seen positively by others, and, from the negative perspective, to avoid a threat to our "face" and social status. As the game of life involves the use of flattery to gain trust and to achieve certain aims, a basic distrust of flattery may serve as an iron dome against manipulators. However, a counterstrategy, wisely identified by Shakespeare, is to deny our susceptibility to flattery, a paradoxical move that is flattering and antiflattering at the same time.

This process teaches us a lesson about the narcissistic personality. The narcissist is nurtured not by simple flattery, although he may find it extremely pleasant, but by his *denial of his susceptibility to flattery* or *to any other human weakness*. In other words, the narcissist who has been described as highly sensitive to threat to status is the one who is wearing the mask of the *Übermensch*—the "superman"—who is immune to human weakness. He is a person-in-transition, moving from a "form" of weakness and threat to status into the form of the superman. From the "experiment" of *Julius Caesar* conducted in Shakespeare's laboratory, we learn that narcissism is not a static personality type or trait but primarily the way in which *human beings who are status threatened deny their human weakness* and when fighting with this conflict wear a mask that transforms them into an *Übermensch*. As we also learn, narcissism is a continuous dimension of transformation and not a well-demarcated category.

When sent on a "hunting mission," our intelligence agent may approach certain people who are sensitive to status and are sure of their inborn immunity to manipulation. Interacting with these people, our nonjudgmental agent may gain their trust by praising their impressive immunity to flattery in particular and to human weakness in general. As we can learn from the play, Decius' allegedly simple strategy worked well and Caesar the great is led to the trap like an elephant marching into a deadly trench. It is trivial that even Caesar—the great vulture—is not immune to flattery, but Shakespeare's lesson is that the higher is the flying vulture, the more it is prone to flattery and its deadly consequences.

BUT CAESAR IS NOT A STUPID GENERAL

In contrast with the image of Caesar as a hard-headed general, Caesar himself identifies the potential threat emerging from his "colleagues" and suspects Cassius on the grounds that "he thinks too much. Such men are dangerous." The idea that people, like Cassius, who "think too much" are dangerous is of interesting diagnostic value. According to Caesar, there are several more reasons to suspect Cassius as he

1. has a lean and hungry look;
2. thinks and reads too much;
3. is a great observer;
4. is too thin;
5. loves no plays;
6. hears no music; and
7. seldom smiles.

For Caesar, people like Cassius (and Brutus), who are not "sports," who are too reflective, who have an ascetic appearance, who are not extravert or sociable, and who are emotionally restrained and fail to smile from the heart, are a source of concern. These are introverts who, as we have learned, have no basic trust in others and turn into themselves to find a solution to threats.

In contrast to Caesar's earlier presentation as a narcissist who falls prey to simple flattery, he is now portrayed as much more clever than we conceived him before and seems to be insightful in his diagnostic intuition. From Caesar's diagnosis, we cannot learn that football fans or those who enjoy beer and pub songs are the most trustworthy guys. However, we learn to suspect people who prefer rigid and *abstract* moral norms to real-world and concrete concerns and understand that those who can never be *satisfied* by simple means cannot be trusted in a dynamic and adaptive social system.

It seems that the interests of these personas lie in a kind of abstract transcendental realm far beyond the web of interests and motives that constitutes the basic human trust and threat systems. These are the people who love humanity more than human beings and who may be blind to the suffering of particular human beings by justifying it as a sacrifice that is always secondary to the great cause.

This attitude is evident when Brutus dissembles by saying,

> We all stand up against the spirit of Caesar,
> And in the spirit of men there is no blood.

This is of course far from the truth. While Brutus would like the conspirators to be conceived as "sacrificers" rather than as "butchers," it is the actual bloody manslaughter that determines their appropriate title. Brutus, who adopts a copying mechanism of detachment, which is characteristic of the obsessive personality, would like us to believe that, as the conspirators stand against the "spirit of Caesar" and as there is no blood in spirit, their bloody deed is not bloody at all. He realizes of course that murdering Caesar is a bloody deed but then urges his coconspirators to do it without anger or vengeful appearance as if there were nothing personal and emotional about it.

Indeed, acknowledging that the spirit has a corpse attached to it and that this corpse bleeds when stabbed and cries for help in agony when wounded is a troubling issue, but even this issue can be dismissed by Brutus proposing an emotionless and businesslike kind of murder. We can see how the personality of Brutus, the honorable citizen, defends itself against the full realization of its bloody deed by adopting a perspective that prioritizes the abstract ideal over the concrete human and detaches the emotion from its embodied context. Caesar was right in his diagnosis, as those who love humanity more than human beings should be a major source of concern.

Brutus urges his coconspirators to see themselves as sacrificers and surgeons rather than as butchers and murderers. Indeed, conceiving themselves as worshiping God (or the gods) and as the healers of society is whitewashing that is supposed to remove the spots of blood from the murderers' togas. What bothers Brutus most seems to be the *cleanliness* of the deed rather than its moral essence. This is something that clearly echoes the obsessive/anal personality presented above. It is a personality organized around the threat of *contagion*. Brutus is not so much concerned about the subordination of his status by Caesar as he is concerned by Caesar's potential *metaphorical contamination* of Rome's beauty as an ideal. Contagion is deeply associated with purity and purity is deeply associated with sexuality. In modern terms, we may suspect that Brutus is a hidden fascist who cares about the sexual purity of Rome, the motherland.

Brutus's internal conflict is another aspect of his indecisive anal personality and he is even tortured before the murder takes place. In Act 2 Scene 1, he says,

> Between the acting of a dreadful thing
> And the first motion, all the interim is
> Like a phantasma or a hideous dream.

Following the planning of the murder, Brutus experiences a kind of daydreaming. He has lost a well-established connection with reality and suffers from dissociation. This is the *freezing response* that we have discussed before. Is he really suffering or does he just want to maintain his persona of a moralist struggling with the inevitable pain of the moral deed? This is a question to be seriously considered, but first let us return to Caesar and his personality.

NO FEAR! CAESAR AND COURAGE

Caesar's occupation with courage is not a simple issue. At the opening of Act 2 Scene 2, when during a troubled night his wife cries out in her sleep, "They murder Caesar!" he sends his servant to the priests to "present a sacrifice." His alleged certainty in his success is probably a cover to hide his fears, but, when asked by his wife to stay at home, he declares that the "things" that threaten him will vanish when they see his face, that "cowards die many times" while the "valiant never taste of death but once," that Caesar is more dangerous than danger, that he is a "lion," and so on. Narcissism is first and foremost the ultimate denial of our human weakness in front of others and aims to defend us from threats to our social status. Caesar, who is denying his human weakness and presenting himself as a god-man, like Stalin the "Iron Man," is actually triggering the fear of his people of the threat of being subordinated to this god-like persona. Like the dialectics of slave and master, masochist and sadist, the narcissist has no independent existence separated from a cheering audience admiring and celebrating the superiority of the *Übermensch* while at the same time sharpening its knifes for the appropriate moment. Therefore, the complementary aspect of the narcissistic admiration is the ever-experienced threat of the god-man.

The human fear of god-like men can be better comprehended by reading a beautiful poem by the Polish poet (and priest) Jan Twardowski. The poem is titled "The World" (2015) and it starts with "God hid himself so that the world could be seen." Twardowski explains to us that, if he had not hidden himself, God would have filled our presence to a degree where it would have been impossible to notice little creatures like the ant (or human beings). A god-like man is not hidden like god. Therefore, his presence does not leave a space for the existence of others unless they seek to disappear in his grandiosity, as sometimes happens to the mob cheering for the dictator. If God had not been hidden and the ant had not been conscious, the ant would probably have rebelled against God. In the context of the god-like man, it is clear that he usurps the place of others and therefore their fear is justified.

In contrast with his pompous image, when Decius comes to take Caesar to the senate, our "lion" refuses to come, justifying his avoidance through Calpurnia's dream of his death. Decius is clearly attuned to the narcissistic personality of Caesar, who is immersed on one hand in fears and uncertainty and on the other hand in a grandiose sense of himself as a lion of which even danger is frightened.

Instead of rejecting Calpurnia's dream in a straightforward manner, Decius proposes a different interpretation of her dream that flatters Caesar's grandiose sense of self, an interpretation that is warmly embraced by Caesar, who renounces his wife's worries: "How foolish do your fears seem now, Calpurnia!" Caesar's grandiose, albeit shaky, sense of self appears later when he describes himself as "constant as the Northern Star," an unshakable personality like Mount Olympus, and emphasizes his *uniqueness* in the world: "but one in all." The point when Caesar compares himself to Olympus, the house of the gods, is *precisely* the point when the conspirators stab him to death. At the height of his narcissism, at a point when he associates himself with the gods, Caesar is touching the conspirators' deepest fear of a god-like emperor.

For Cassius, the arrogant manipulator, this is a point where his own narcissism is threatened the most. For Brutus, the moralist, it is the point where his sense of justice is threatened the most. For Cassius the narcissist, Caesar's death is an event to be remembered for generations to come, together with his own courageous act. For Brutus, it should signal cries of "Peace, freedom and liberty!" As we can see, the coalition of two different personalities—Brutus the over-moralist and Cassius the narcissist—has crystallized into the orchestrated assassination of Caesar.

POSTMORTEM

The events that take place after Caesar's assassination strengthen our understanding of the characters' personalities. Brutus, the rigid moralist, fails to see the way in which Antony plans to turn against them, while Cassius, the suspicious manipulator, is well aware of the danger facing them. When Brutus is trying to justify the assassination to the Romans, he mistakenly turns to reason and morality: "not that I loved Caesar less, but that I loved Rome more." The crowd cheers "Live, Brutus!" but the mob is an unstable system and things turn upside down for Brutus.

Antony's speech is a model of persuasive rhetoric that can be summed up as an intelligent appeal to emotion. While as an obsessive personality Brutus appeals to the crowd's *reason* and avoids an encounter with emotions, Antony appeals to the audience's emotions, for instance, by pointing to Caesar's empathy with the Romans ("When that the poor have cried, Caesar hath wept"), evoking their deep emotions ("If you have tears, prepare to shed them now"), and turning the plebeians against the conspirators. Antony, in fact, uses the same trick used by Decius. Instead of presenting a simple and explicit argument that may confront Brutus's own speech and be suspected as manipulative, he paradoxically declares that his aim *is not* persuasive:

> I come not, friends, to steal away your hearts.
> I am no orator, as Brutus is.

This is a clear rhetorical trick that gains the crowd's trust and paves the way to the emotional incitement against the conspirators.

Human communication moves in circular, or more exactly spiral, motions in which the different levels interact in an interesting way (Bateson, 1972/2000). As illustrated by Rene Magritte's famous painting *Ceci n'est pas une pipe*, language signifies the world while recursively qualifying its signifying power. Antony's act of persuasion gains its power from denying itself as an act of persuasion, in the same way as Decius's denial of Caesar's vulnerability to flattery is in itself an act of flattery.

In this context, we may better understand Brutus's obsessive personality, which is characterized not only by adherence to rigid moral norms and by appeal to reason and avoidance of the emotional aspect of the human mind but also by its inability *to understand and manipulate the recursive aspect of human psychology*, which is crucial for gaining trust for deceptive aims and for defending against such attempts. In other words, *what characterizes Brutus's "rigid" personality is the inability to think paradoxically and in a spiral kind of way*. For Brutus, as the earth was for the ancients, the human psyche is a flat surface standing on the back of reason, and whose boundaries cannot be traversed except at the price of falling into the void.

Brutus's rigid personality paradoxically leads to his criticism by Cassius as a wrongdoer, the most painful criticism that can be launched against him. When Brutus meets Cassius on their way to confront Antony's forces, the first thing said by Cassius is "You have done me wrong." This criticism shocks Brutus, who cannot believe that he has done wrong even to his enemies. Guilty feelings are again evoked.

The wrongdoing described by Cassius concerns Lucius Pella, who has been accused by Brutus of taking bribery while Cassius considers him innocent. This is a minor issue, of course, but Cassius seems to be angry with Brutus for dealing with such a matter at an inappropriate time ("In such a time as this"), when they are fighting for their lives. Brutus the overmoralist cannot accept the idea that morality is context-dependent and accuses Cassius of corruption, escalating his accusations to the point where the two turn into bitter enemies. Stalin was right in getting rid of his own Brutus (Trotsky); by adopting the most noble and sacred norms of morality, Brutus finds not a single decent man, *including himself*. At this point, we may understand why the ultimate moralist is always afflicted by guilt and regret. As no one is perfect, to include the moralist, and as being imperfect implies being immoral, there is no escape from guilt and self-destruction. To recall, the obsessive personality is guided by the fear of contagion and by the emotion of disgust. In contrast with other sources of threat, contagion is clearly a slippery slope, as bacteria exist everywhere even in our own body, where they have an indispensable function. Ultimate purity is therefore an ideal that contradicts life itself and necessarily leads to self-annihilation.

Cassius's rage does not threaten Brutus ("For I am armed so strong with honesty") while Brutus's moral zealousness shocks Cassius ("A friend should bear his friend's infirmities/But Brutus makes mine greater than they are"). Indeed, no one is perfect, and friends are supposed to know it, but the over-moralists, such as Brutus, have no friends, except for Lady Justice.

Finally, Brutus calms down, explaining to Cassius that for a moment he forgot his Stoic philosophy as a result of his deep sorrow upon his wife's suicide. Indeed, losing one's temper is an embarrassing situation for the anal personality. Brutus's justification, though, is an excuse. Grief can have several expressions that are indicative of our personality but Brutus chooses the expression that perfectly fits his overall pattern of relating to the world. It was Bakhtin (1990) who insightfully proposed that there is "no alibi in existence," as every deed is performed by a unique individual who holds a unique perspective on existence and who cannot escape the responsibility of wrongdoing. Brutus's "alibi in existence" is the general and abstract ideal of Rome. However, deep in his heart, he is tortured by the murder, and this finally leads to his self-annihilation by suicide. His conflict and pain are other characteristics of the obsessive/anal personality. Death is around the corner and Brutus, the ultimate moralist, is on his way to meet Lady Justice, who, like him, is armed with honesty but unfortunately blind.

DISCUSSION: WHAT HAVE WE LEARNED ABOUT PERSONALITY FROM *JULIUS CAESAR*?

First, let us remember several lessons we have learned from the play:

- The narcissist is characterized by the ultimate denial of human weakness in an attempt to manage threats to his status. In a circular way, he forms his narcissistic image in reference to others.
- The obsessive personality prefers abstract moral norms of purity to the concrete, dirty, and "contaminated" human deed.
- The obsessive personality fails to understand the recursive–hierarchical nature of human personality.

Now, let us discuss the importance of literature for understanding personalities, but this time through another artistic medium, which is the cinema. In the wonderful film *Caesar Must Die*, directed by the Taviani brothers, a group of real prisoners from Rebibbia prison in Italy are performing *Julius Caesar*. This movie therefore presents a plot (i.e., the play) within a plot (i.e., the film). There are rare moments in the film where the two plots intersect. In one of the scenes, described above, Cassius is seducing Brutus to join the conspiracy against Caesar. In the film, the scene is played by two prisoners while a third prisoner is present in the same room playing cards. When Cassius is asking Brutus to trust him, the third prisoner bursts into the dialogue by bitterly uttering something like "See where I've come as a result of trusting other people." The prisoner's comment is a warning signal to the character of Brutus. It is a comment made by a real prisoner (albeit a player in a movie) who has lived real systems of trust and distrust, to a fictive character invented by Shakespeare hundreds of years ago and tragically captured in a fictive world. Even if he were played a million times on stages all over the world, Brutus would be doomed to follow the imperative of his personality, to obey his destiny, and to murder Caesar. In contrast, the prisoner commenting on the scene is a human being who is destined to live his life only once but with a sense of freedom, otherwise his bitter comment would have made no sense. After all, what is the point in advising a fictive character unless you (hopelessly) aim to change his course of behavior? The prisoner could have said to Brutus that he understands Brutus's strive for justice and that he greatly appreciates the fact that Brutus is ready to sacrifice his life for a just ideal. However, the prisoner would have also told Brutus that he—as an outside observer of the play—knows that Brutus's loved wife will commit suicide, that Brutus himself will commit suicide, and that the next governors of Rome will be no better than Caesar. With his outside perspective, the prisoner would have questioned the way Brutus's obsessive and overmoralist character should be manifested in practice. He could have advised Brutus to follow his deep sense of justice and reject Cassius's proposal to join the conspiracy, explaining to him that the moral act is sometimes to avoid rigid and abstract norms in favor of a sensitive reading of the real-life situation with its in-built dirtiness.

The prisoner's comment echoes the feelings of some people who watch the play, who wish to warn Brutus the nobleman against joining a conspiracy that will finally lead to no good. However, in the Shakespearean laboratory of human personality, there is no freedom from behaving as one is. Brutus, the anal character, lacks the spiral way of thinking, the *Ceci n'est pas une pipe* kind of wisdom that might help him to position himself as a free man rather than as a fictive character. Those who remain outside the play, observing it with great excitement, are left to ponder whether they have freedom or whether they are too the players on a stage observed by others. While the philosophical question of whether we have freedom of choice is unresolved, the psychological answer is more encouraging. Observing the play as outsiders, we may want to adopt the same stance and observe our thoughts, emotions, and behavior as if they were a play and ask ourselves whether we are the slaves of certain patterns of thought, behavior, and emotions (i.e., personalities) that may push us off a cliff. Adopting this stance, whether or not it is epistemologically grounded, is an act of freedom.

This book's introduction suggests that literature, as a laboratory of human experience, is the needle that stitches the abstractness of our theories to human personalities *in vivo*. Real life is sometimes conceived like Borges's garden of the forking paths (Borges, 2010), a realm of possibilities where each choice made at a crossroad will put us on a totally different trajectory. Shakespeare's play, as an experiment whose results are consistent across numerous replications, is in contrast a realm of actualities in which the characters cannot escape their destiny. The power of literature is in providing us with a *loophole* perspective stretching from the garden of the forking paths into the laboratory of Dr. Shakespeare.

Between the garden of the forking paths and Shakespeare's laboratory, the contemplating observer may keep asking himself, "What is the meaning of having a personality?"

NOTE

1. See Patenaude (2010) for a detailed description of Trotsky and his personality.

Chapter Six

King Lear

On Flattery, Grooming, and Treason

King Lear shares his inheritance among his daughters by measuring and paying for their degree of flattery. In this chapter, I aim to show how flattery is grounded in the practice of social grooming and how the narcissistic personality is deeply related to flattering. Reading Shakespeare suggests some insights into the narcissistic personality and why the "madman is the king who considers himself a king" (Lacan cited in Žižek, 2006).

Lear, the king of Britain, decides to divide his kingdom among his three daughters: Goneril, Regan, and Cordelia. He invites his daughters to a meeting and explains his decision as an attempt "to shake all cares and business" and to allow himself to "crawl toward death." The specific situation in which the king and his daughters attend is explained as an attempt to prevent "future strife."

Our first impression, therefore, is of an old king who is seeking to retire and to deliver the burden of governing his kingdom to the next generation. He invites his daughters to visit him so that he can announce the shares of their heritage to prevent future disputes. Up to now, Lear is reasonable. However, what he says next creates a sharp turn in the plot and an interesting equation:

> Which of you shall say doth love us most,
> That we our largest bounty may extend

The equation laid out by Lear is simple: The bounty each daughter will get is a direct function of the love that she shows to her old father. As we will later see, the relationship between the size of the bounty and the size of the love showed by each daughter is not a smooth mathematical function but based on a binary logical decision, as a daughter who refuses to express her love will get nothing. However, let us leave mathematical and logical particularities aside, and dwell deeper into Lear's personality.

In his introduction to the annotated version of *King Lear*, Burton Raffel (Shakespeare, 2007, p. xxii) suggests that "His [Lear's] plan to give up power and divide his kingdom among his children seems business like and feasible—until this curiously bland idiocy." Describing Lear's behavior as "idiocy" or "foolishness" (Shakespeare, 2007, p. xxii) may be a justified value judgment but, as psychologists, our perspective should be different even from the neuropsychological explanation of Lear's behavior (i.e., Alzheimer) later proposed by Burton Raffel.

First, we must realize that Lear does not simply "plan to give up power," as suggested by Raffel. By asking his daughters to *prove* their love and to *compete* for their father's love, Lear is giving up his kingdom for a *substitute*: his daughters' love. Giving up power is therefore compensated by gaining another power through his daughters' love. As we can see, and as we learned in the first part of this book, *human psychology has a deep semiotic aspect in which meaning/value is formed through symbolic exchange and substitute*. In our case, it is the exchange: love for a kingdom. This is a very important point that will be theoretically elaborated later, where another famous substitute (i.e., a pound of flesh for money) will be the focus of our reading.

As we learn from the classic work of Ferdinand de Saussure (1993), a meaning-making or value system, whether economic or psychological, is a system of exchange and substitutes. Richard III desperately asks to substitute his kingdom for a horse; Shylock demands the substitute of a pound of flesh for Antonio's debt; and Lear asks for his daughters' love as a substitute for the kingdom he plans to give them. Our systems of substitutions, exchanges, and values are therefore crucial to understanding our *meaning-making systems* and how we are related to the world of others, hence our personalities.

What can we learn about a man who is asking to substitute his kingdom for love? Specifically, for the love of his daughters? We can intuitively evoke the metaphor "love is like a kingdom" and hypothesize that, just as Lear governs his kingdom, he would like to govern his daughters' love. Indeed, the whole, and one even may say embarrassing, situation in which his daughters are asked to show their love is a scenario of control and possession, as if true love, rather than flattery, can be possessed by someone or triggered by authority and command. All this interpretation is valid given the existence of "true love," a concept that might be incompatible with Lear's cultural norms.

The second hypothesis that we may immediately propose is that Lear is what we have called a narcissist. A narcissist is a person who struggles with a threat to status by "forgetting" his human qualities and constituting a superficial image of an *Übermensch* through a distorted mirror image of his relations with others and his own self. Lear, whose *Übermensch* status is nurtured through governing his kingdom, clearly understands that giving up his kingdom is giving up his status and, as we can hypothesize, giving up his (false) self. As such, Lear asks for valuable compensation—a substitute that will allow him to maintain his grandiose sense of self or at least to "crawl to death" with a sense of value.

While we as outside observers seem—like Burton Raffel—to be shocked by Lear's "idiocy," it seems that for his oldest daughter, Goneril, there is nothing more natural than providing her father with a grandiose reflection of his self through words of flattery. Indeed, without a wasted moment of hesitation, she responds to her father's demand with the rhetoric of flattery, describing her love for her father as "Beyond what can be valued." This exaggerated flattering paradoxically encapsulates the seed of annihilation, as something that is "Beyond what can be valued" is something that exists outside our value and meaning-making system, and as such it is *meaningless*. Indeed, Goneril offers to her father meaningless love and teaches us that, from a psychological semiotic perspective, *that which is beyond measure is actually meaningless*. This is an interesting point that also appears in one of the Shakespeare's other plays *Much Ado About Nothing*. In one of this play's scenes, we meet Don John, who is the villain of the play (emphasis mine):

Conrade: What the goodyear, my lord! Why are you thus *out of measure* sad?

Don John: There is *no measure* in the occasion that breeds, therefore the sadness is *without limit*.

We can see that, in this play too, one of the characters speaks about a limitless and immeasurable emotion, in this case sadness. As it is immeasurable and without limit, it is actually a meaningless emotion that seems to be a rhetorical expression, or, according to a much more disturbing interpretation, a slip into the unconscious realm, which is characterized according to Matte-Blanco (1975) by being limitless and measureless. In our case, Don John "experiences" a limitless emotion as a justification for his planned vicious deed. Now let us return to Lear and the meaningless love proposed by his daughter.

The aforementioned interpretation is in perfect line with our understanding of the narcissistic personality, which is nurtured by and maintains its value through a *false image*. However, let us not understand this personality in terms of nouns and "reification" (Billig 2013) but through the verbs of common language. Lear is a *king* who is intentionally ready to give up his status. This is not a trivial situation for a king in a nondemocratic society. The king's status is a shaky business. After all, the king is made of flesh and blood. In wearing the narcissistic mask, Lear is involved in transformation, as proposed by Bakhtin, a transformation from low to high status; but, when he gives up his kingdom, the transformation works in the opposite direction, leaving him "bare and naked," to use the Biblical phrase. This situation is threatening and the way this threat is resolved is through a substitute, which is—like any other kind of substitute—a faked image, as the substitute is never the thing it substitutes. This point can be better clarified as we keep reading the play, specifically if we take into account the wider concept of "social grooming."

Reading Goneril's flattering words, the modern reader, specifically the modern American reader, cannot avoid using the term "ass kissing." While this slang term has negative connotations, it clearly echoes the evolutionary roots of flattery in social grooming. In other words, while Goneril is making her best efforts to flatter her father to gain a larger share of his kingdom, she is also echoing the practice of social grooming, well grounded in her evolutionary history as well as in the particular discursive style used to approach kings.

Social grooming is "an activity in which individuals in a group clean or maintain one another's body or appearance" (Wikipedia). A cat licking its fur is involved in personal grooming but a cat licking its kitten is involved in social grooming. Social grooming is not a trivial act of cleaning per se. In fact, and like many other processes we conceive as "personal" or "individualistic," it *ontogenetically* originates in the *social realm* and is internalized into the personal realm. The kitten licked by its mother learns to turn its mother's love into "personal grooming" and self-love, which is described as healthy narcissism. Here it starts to be clear how social grooming is linked to narcissism and to narcissism's personality dimension. However, let me elaborate the cat's case through a specific example.

Many years ago, my children adopted a cat and found after a couple of days that, though she looked extremely young and small, she was the mother of two kittens. After the cat family came to live in our house, their behavior turned into an object of scientific observation and a constant source of interest, pleasure, empathy, and reflection. One day, I learned how the mother cat was weaning its kittens from breastfeeding. One of the two kittens was trying to approach the cat's nipples to gain access to his favorite food. The mother, who was lying on the floor, pushed the kitten's head with her feet, removing the kitten from the source of libidinal pleasure. However, while pushing the kitten away, the cat did another thing: As her feet pushed the kitten, they grasped its head, in a clinch wrestling position, and then she *licked* the kitten's head! It was as if the mother cat was saying,

Listen my dear son, from now on you cannot enjoy breastfeeding but have to feed yourself on solid food that doesn't provide the same pleasure. As a substitute, I give you something else, which is the joy of social grooming. I licked your head, and, when you lick yourself from now on, you will recall your mother's love and care. And remember, my son, to read Freud in order to learn that self-love, which is crucial for a healthy and happy life, always emerges from the love of others.

This example and imagined speech clearly illustrate the psychological significance of social grooming and its deep connection with (healthy) narcissism. Grooming has a hygienic function but also a psychological function related to *care*. The psychological and the social cannot be artificially separated, as we have already realized.

Grooming has clear social functions among primates, such as the increase of social bonds (Dunbar, 2010). According to Seyfarth (1977), grooming, at least as studied among female primates, is offered in return for benefits best provided by the highest-ranking females. It means that grooming is more profitable when offered to a higher-ranked member of the group. If we consider flattery to be an abstraction of social grooming, it is clear why flattery is targeted at kings or at peers of the same social status. It is hard to imagine what reason we would have to flatter our subordinates, although in modern democratic societies, this situation has changed. Today, it is common to observe a boss grooming his employees to gain their collaboration. Therefore, flattery is functional in maintaining social status and gaining goods in return for future benefits. In this context, Goneril's flattery of Lear is crystal clear. It is a cultural form of discourse that is grounded in our cognitive-biological roots and our healthy narcissism.

While the benefits of social grooming may be clear at first glance, they are less clear in an uncertain world where there is always the chance of cheating and exploitation and where flattery will not necessarily pay off. Things become complex when they are lifted from their original cognitive-biological context into the social-symbolic realm. In this context, social grooming may be discussed through the "raise-the-stakes" strategy (Roberts & Sherrat, 1998). This strategy describes a dynamic in which the interacting agents incrementally increase their investment in the interaction if the other side matches or betters its interlocutor's last move. This strategy may be highly effective in a context where the cost is immediate and the benefit is delayed or not secured. For example, one study found that male chimpanzees involved in social grooming employed the raise-the-stakes strategy during *social instability* but not under other conditions (Kaburu & Newton-Fisher, 2013). The reason for this interesting finding is that, in a context of social instability, one cannot easily trust one's partner and therefore investing in social grooming may be a costly activity that may bring no benefits. In this evolutionary context, Lear's demand for "social grooming" is wrong as he assumes that his relationship with his daughters is an *all-or-nothing* affair where there is no place for trust violation. Lear fails to understand the *instability* of his status as a king who is giving up his power and exposing himself to trust violation by his flattering daughters, as indeed happens in the play.

Narcissists such as Lear or Julius Caesar are always surprised by trust violation and treason as they adopt an all-or-nothing strategy instead of understanding the unstable nature of life and adopting a more cautious trust strategy such as raise the stakes. This is an important point about the cognitive aspect of narcissism and the narcissistic assessment of the threat-to-status situation. The narcissist is an all-or-nothing person as his false self-image is of stability and grandiosity.

Learning a lesson from the grooming chimpanzees, Lear could have incrementally given up his power in exchange for solid signs of love and loyalty from his daughters, signs that guaranteed his future position as a retired king. However, this lesson would probably have fallen on deaf ears. For the narcissist, recognizing the instability, or more accurately the vicissitudes, of life is realizing one's own weakness and fragility as a human being who may be exposed to cheating even by those to whom one is closest. Such a realization is too painful for the god-like man, who lives with the false image of an omnipotent and omniscient self. It is trivial to understand why at the same time Lear is status threatened and blind to the threat of status. People of high social status are less threatened by social evaluation and therefore are supposed to be less prone to monitoring their behavior, as recently found by Boksem, Kostermans, Milivojevic, and De Cremer (2012). Therefore, we can understand why Lear does not suspect his daughters or himself. After all, he is *THE king*. However, social status is not only an external mark; it may also be a highly conflictual psychological perspective. The narcissist can never be fully assured about his status as the threat to status is the main axis of his personality. Lear is seeking a confirmation of his status. As such, he is status threatened. At the same time, he adopts the all-or-nothing strategy, which indicates his blindness to the status threat. These conflicting behaviors are a clear indication of the conflict that constitutes the narcissistic personality (McWilliams, 2011, 2012).

At this point, it is important to re-emphasize that, among human beings, grooming is not merely physical but also social. Among the most salient social grooming methods, one can find (Fu & Lee, 2007, p. 255):

1. opinion conformity (e.g., "You're right, boss"),
2. rendering favors (e.g., "Boss, I bought you something nice in Vegas"),
3. downward self-presentation (e.g., "Sir, I'm just a student who hasn't learned enough"),
4. verbal and nonverbal dissemblance (e.g., "You look gorgeous"), and
5. flattery ("You are the greatest").

In fact, Fu and Lee (2007) found that even preschoolers are sensitive to the use of flattery, showing how early we become socialized for grooming. All the aforementioned grooming behaviors are evident in the interaction between Lear and his flattering daughters. Regan, his second daughter, follows Goneril's footsteps by flattering to her father, and when it is the turn of Cordelia (the youngest daughter), we expect to observe the same pattern of flattery. However, our expectation is refuted and this refutation generates dramatic tension.

Turning to Cordelia, Lear challenges her to meet the same high standards set by her sisters:

> What can you say to draw
> A third more opulent than your sisters? Speak.

Cordelia's response is shocking: "Nothing, my lord." Lear the narcissist cannot believe this answer and threatens his daughter: "Nothing will come of nothing, speak again." However, Cordelia refuses to take part in this narcissistic celebration of her father's grandiosity. She refuses to flatter beyond her "bond" or duty. Here we seem to sense the appearance of a personality type we have met before. Can you guess what it is?

While Goneril and Regan understand their father's narcissistic personality and feel comfortable in celebrating his narcissism for the benefit of the kingdom, Cordelia is motivated by her rigid moral standards regardless of the price she may pay for her ideals. Lear acknowledges his daughter's rigid personality by saying "So young, and so untender [tough]?" Cordelia responds by saying "So young, my lord, and true." Indeed, for Cordelia, like for Brutus in Julius Caesar, Lady Justice is the only acceptable moral compass to guide her behavior. For the "obsessive" personality, the guiding compass is the perfect and "clean" world of ideals, which is remote from the polluted and repugnant true world in which the obsessive has no interest in taking part. Instead of just fitting herself to her father's needs, Cordelia brutally confronts his narcissism by exposing it as a lie, diametrically opposed to her guiding truth. This approach is a serious blow to the king's narcissism. In addition, this approach is a blow to the essence of human politeness. Removing the masks of behavior is removing the cloth of human civilization or even the cloth of the most basic social interactions. Cordelia's behavior is another indication of the way in which the logic of morality conflicts with the logic of life to a level where it threatens life itself.

Lear's response is to form another substitute "Let it be so, thy truth then be thy dower," which means that, instead of getting one-third of the kingdom as her dowry, Cordelia will have to settle for her truth as her dowry. Lear is thus getting even, like other narcissists we meet in Shakespeare's plays. He is getting even metaphorically but literally too, as he gives Cordelia a "measure for measure"—the name of one of Shakespeare's plays. By removing his parental care from Cordelia, Lear gives expression to his "narcissistic rage." In fact, he presents himself as a "dragon" and Cordelia as a "wrath." Is there a more appropriate way for the king to describe his narcissist rage than portraying it as a "dragon"?

In trying to preserve his grandiose sense of self as the king through the substitute of his daughters' "love," Lear encounters resistance from his young and beloved daughter—he says "I love her most" and describes her as "our joy." While Lear sees Cordelia's behavior as shameful, the King of France is charmed by this young, obsessive lady and takes her under his patronage. At this point, we may understand that *an interaction between a narcissist and an overmoralist, or the obsessive personality, is a recipe for disaster*. The reason is simple. The narcissist feels status threatened. As such, he seeks social approval by motivating others to mirror his allegedly grandiose self, through various practices of social grooming of which flattery is the most noticeable. The overmoralist is not a suitable partner in this kind of interaction as he is motivated by the ideal of truth while the narcissist's reflected image is, vitally, a lie.

The Earl of Kent is another overmoralist who refuses to take a part in the narcissistic celebration:

> Think'st thou that duty shall have dread [i.e., must be afraid] to speak,
> When power to flattery bows?

It is interesting that Kent, the first to put Lear in his place, uses the word "duty," a term that is appealing to overmoralists. His opening remark immediately tags the Earl of Kent as the second potential obsessive personality in the play. Indeed, he is threatened by Lear and responds by saying, "My life I never held but as a pawn." For Kent, life is just a temporary pawn given to him "To wage against my enemies." Life is a weapon used for war against enemies, and therefore one does not have to fear losing it. We can see that Cordelia the overmoralist is not afraid of losing her father's patronage and dowry for the sake of "truth" while Kent is not afraid of losing his life for the sake of "duty," as life is only a weapon in the service of the great justice. While Shakespeare recruits our sympathy to the just couple, Cordelia and Kent, we must reflectively and critically analyze their characters. Cordelia refuses to provide her father with his "substitute." The result is that, given his fear of the status threat, he experiences *horror vacui*. He is left with a sense of emptiness without being able to maintain his status. This is a cruel act done for the sake of morality only.

Kent, who supports Cordelia's stance, is also blind to the old man's fears and see "duty" as superior to everything else. Can we negotiate with such personas as Cordelia and Kent? In a time of war, one would like to see these characters standing by one's side, bravely fighting for the just cause, as finally happens in the play. However, in days of peace, one might find them to be intolerable and a zealous threat to the natural flow of life with its social grooming and unjustified flattery.

"AND YOUR LARGE SPEECHES MAY YOUR DEEDS APPROVE"

Being threatened by Lear, who is unable to accept his criticism, Kent is forced to leave, not before approaching Goneril and Regan and saying, "And your large [i.e., lavish] speeches may your deeds approve." As we realized in reading *Julius Caesar*, the obsessive personality finds it difficult to deal with language's sneaky behavior and its treacherous relationship with the world of deeds. An obsessive is someone who means what he says, says what he means, and does what he says. This is true for Cordelia, who admits that she lacks the "oily art" "To speak and purpose not."

This ideal synchronization between intention, words, and deeds is of minor relevance for Goneril and Regan, who dislike the attempt of their overmoralistic sister to preach to them: "Prescribe not us our duties." As we can see, the overmoralist is always eager to tell others what is right and what is wrong and to force them to take the stairway to heaven. As expected, other people do not like these overmoralists as the overmoralists reflect to others an impaired self that is not in line with their positive self-image.

Goneril and Regan are concerned with more practical issues. They realize that their father's behavior is unstable, that he has "poor judgment," and they are afraid that they will suffer from "unruly waywardness" (i.e., egocentricity), which is a typical characteristic of the narcissist. They do not feel deep sympathy for his behavior and consider his rejection of Cordelia as an indication that he cannot be trusted.

Interestingly, Lear is not the only old man who is manipulated in the play. The Earl of Gloucester has two sons. His bastard son, Edmund, fakes a letter from his older brother, Edgar, in which Edgar allegedly proposes to kill the old earl in return for "half his revenue." Gloucester questions the authenticity of the letter by asking Edmund whether he identifies his brother's handwriting. Edmund manipulates Gloucester through soft words: "It is his hand, my lord. But I hope his heart is not in the contents." The ease with which Gloucester is misled into the trench is shocking and he impulsively describes Edgar as

"Abhorred [disgusting] villain! Unnatural, detested, brutish [savage] villain." However, a couple of lines later, he says, "He cannot be such a monster."

What can we learn about a person who can be so easily incited against his own son? Gloucester, like Lear and Julius Caesar, can be easily manipulated and betrayed by those he trusts most. In fact, Lear and Gloucester have a trust issue. For them, *trust is a matter of all or none*. Lear trusts Goneril and Regan but distrusts his beloved daughter Cordelia. Gloucester trusts his bastard son, Edmund, and does not question his motives, while impulsively suspecting his true son, Edgar.

In Gloucester case, there is a "priming" effect of the situation to which he was a witness at Lear's court. Gloucester cannot believe that the king has given up his power. He is in emotional turmoil and, when presented with the letter by Edmund, he is already primed to expect the worse. Therefore, his interpretation of Edgar's alleged letter is based on his emotional distress, leaving the appropriate judgment aside. After sending Edmund to find Edgar, Gloucester ponders the situation, locating it in a wider apocalyptic context in which the old order has collapsed, paving the way to emerging chaos. His interpretation of the situation and Edgar's alleged letter could have made a wonderful case study for a cognitive-behavioral psychologist, who might have pointed to Gloucester's self-defeating and distorted thoughts.

The apocalyptic vision portrayed by Gloucester is highly diagnostic as he conceives the world as *aggressive and chaotic*: "Love cools, friendship falls off." This is what we have identified as the paranoid personality, which is organized around the imagined threat of violence by the outside world— violence that is actually the projection of his own aggressive intentions, as is evident in his aggression against his innocent son. The narcissist is manipulated by flattery and the paranoid by an imagined threat. If our intelligence agent wanted to manipulate Gloucester into action, he would only have to trigger Gloucester's fear of annihilating violence. At the same time, our agent would need to be careful in hiding his true intentions by (paradoxically) questioning the aggressive intentions of others—the same intentions that he "exposed" a minute earlier! This is precisely how Edmund manipulates Gloucester, and this is the same "recursive-hierarchical" process that we observed in *Julius Caesar*. Edmund is well aware of the defense mechanism known as "projection":

> we make guilty of our own disaster the sun, the moon and the stars . . . An admirable evasion of whoremaster man, to lay his goatish [lustful] disposition to the charge of a star!

Edmund also manipulates Edgar, by telling him that their father is upset with him and advising Edgar to keep his distance for a while. Edgar understands that "Some villain hath done me wrong" but, like his father, does not identify the villain in his stepbrother. Edgar seems to be a naive person, who "eats" the lies (*lokshen*) fed by his brother. We may hypothesize that Edgar is a trusty fellow to such an extent that he suspects nothing. As Edmund recognizes, his father is "credulous" [over-ready to believe] and his brother "suspects no one;" one is overtrustful and the other is undertrustful. Edmund is revealed over the course of the play as a fearless manipulator who feels no guilt for his actions. He wounds himself and blames Edgar for hurting him.

Let us imagine that Gloucester has some doubts with regard to the integrity of Edmund. He realizes Edmund's lower social status as a bastard can be used against him as a kind of *ad hominem* argument: As he is a bastard, he can be accused of trying to improve his social status by manipulation. However, the fact that Edmund's status can be used against him as a kind of an *ad hominem* argument does not mean that it is actually used against him and that Edmund is just! It is clear that we are in the realm of psychology rather than in the realm of rational argumentation, and Edmund is a villain regardless of the fact that he is a poor bastard.

What is interesting to reveal in Edmund's manipulation of Gloucester is his deep understanding of Gloucester's paranoid personality. The reason is that a paranoid, who projects his own aggression and fears onto others, will be more inclined to accept the possibility that the fact that Edmund is a bastard will be used against him as an *ad hominem* argument. For the paranoid, everything is personal, and Edmund, whether consciously or unconsciously, uses this psychological dynamic in his manipulation of his father.

Edmund is what we would today call a psychopath or antisocial personality. He has no empathy. This is seen later when he says, "The younger rises when the old doth fall." For him, life is a zero-sum game with predators and prey. The younger cannot rise with the old but have to beat them to feel superior and in control. Villains are those who rebel against the old, good social order that has guided human societies since antiquity and Edmund, being a cold-blooded bastard (literally and figuratively) who challenges the most basic social norms, epitomizes the prototype of the villain.

In his famous novel *In Cold Blood* (Capote, 2013), Truman Capote describes a shocking murder that shatters the American public. The title of the novel indicates our repulsion from violence, which is motivated by a lack of emotion. For some reason, we consider a passionate murder to be more "acceptable" than a murder conducted in cold blood. According to some cultural psychological schemes, one cannot argue with emotions but with reason only. A psychopath who operates in cold blood seems to be someone whose reason is deformed. As reason is the hallmark of our superego and of human civilization, we may understand why a cold-blooded villain is such a repulsive character. After all, it is a cold-blooded and manipulative creature, the biblical serpent, that is responsible for our deportation from the Garden of Eden.

THE FOOL AS THE REMOVER OF MASKS

If there is a character who has deep psychological insights in the play, it is Lear's Fool. While presenting your persona is an act of transforming yourself through the use of a mask, the role of the Fool is to remove that mask and expose the negative "face" underneath. In his first appearance in the play, the Fool mirrors Lear's narcissism by saying to Kent, who appears in disguise, "Nay, an [if] thou canst not smile as the wind sits [flatter those in power] thou'lt catch cold shortly." The Fool also suggests that Lear and his daughters have reversed their roles and that "thou madest thy daughters thy mothers." Lear is indeed described by his daughters as a baby who should be both flattered and whipped. The king has therefore turned from a father into a baby and the daughters have turned from children into mothers.

What the Fool teaches Lear is an important lesson about the narcissistic personality. The first lesson is that Lear can be manipulated by flattery and that those who are not willing to provide him with flattery are doomed to "cold." The second important lesson is that narcissistic dynamics involve a threat of moving from one end of a scale to the other without finding a middle point or balance; the king is either a king or a child, without being able to settle himself in between. The fall from the status of king to the status of a needy and helpless baby is characteristic of a narcissistic personality, as is evident in several novels such as *The Count of Monte Cristo* (Dumas, 1910). In contrast with Lear, who is an all-or-nothing personality when it comes to trust, the Fool presents a more skeptical and cautious perspective on human nature and the appropriate suspicion that should probably be felt by a mature and reasonable human being. For example, asking Lear why the nose is located at the middle of the face, the Fool answers, "Why, to keep one's eyes of [i.e., on] either side's nose. That what a man cannot smell out, he may spy into."

Suspicion and the nose are closely related, specifically for the obsessive personality, which is organized around the threat of contagion. For the cynical Fool, the nose should smell out the danger, and, if it cannot smell poisonous relations, such as those between Lear and his daughters, the eyes should help him to "spy into." The "nose" reappears later when the Fool says to Kent, "All that follow their noses are led by their eyes but [i.e., except for] blind men, and there's not a nose among twenty but can smell him that's stinking [i.e., smelling of decay like Lear]." The Fool's nose tells him that Lear is decaying and that Kent (the blind man who cannot "smell" it) is doomed to disaster.

The Fool also provides a critical perspective on Kent's behavior. Kent, as an anal personality, not only echoes his "master's voice" but also zealously expresses his anger at Lear's daughters and their servants. As a result of fighting with Oswald (Goneril's steward), Kent is fetched to the stocks on the order of Cornwall. When Lear and the Fool enter the castle and see Kent in the stocks, the Fool bursts into laughter and says, "When a man's over-lusty at [has too many reasons to escape such as in the case of escaping from a jealous husband] legs, then he wears wooden nether-stocks."

Kent is compared by the Fool to a man who cannot control his sexual urges and is fetched to the stocks as a punishment. This metaphor seems to be incomprehensible as Kent's only sin is in zealously defending his master's honor. However, Kent and a man who cheats with another man's wife have something in common. Both are *motivated by urges rather than by calculated reason*. The cheating man is motivated by his uncontrolled sexual passion, which may lead him to a violent confrontation with other men. Kent is motivated by his uncontrolled passion to do justice, as he sees it. In both cases, the law constraints the passion that threatens to annihilate the existing order, whether that passion is justified or not. In contrast with the image of the obsessive personality as overly rational, we learn from Shakespeare that being unable to control one's rational urges is in deep sense a lack of rationality.

The Fool presents a grounded rational perspective in which a person should cautiously manage his own life and be the captain of his ship. He describes "Fortune" as an "arrant whore" that "Ne'er turns the key [opens its door] to the poor." This means that a person motivated by an unconscious and rigid scheme is actually moved by the illusion of "fortune," which involves an illusory trust in that which can never be trusted if one is not in power. We can see that the Fool is not simply an amusing buffoon who entertains his master. The Fool is the voice of reason, but a voice that others refuse to hear.

Lear's fall is quick to come. In the same scene, when criticized by Goneril for the wild behavior of his people, he experiences a *dissociation*. "Doth any here know me? Why, this is not Lear . . . / Who is it that can tell me who I am?" The Fool is quick to answer: "Lear's shadow." But the "shadow" responds to his daughter's criticism with a burst of narcissistic rage, calling her a "degenerate bastard," a "sea monster," and a "Detested kite [a bird of prey]." He curses Goneril, threatens to hurt himself by plucking out his own eyes, and furiously leaves the palace on his way to his second daughter, only to find his loyal servant—Kent—in the stocks, a situation he conceives as "worse than murder" and a threat to Lear's status ("To do upon respect such violent outrage").

Lear's response is expressed as a psychosomatic pain that he describes as "Hysterica passio." The king, being thrown from his narcissistic position, from his manly status, falls into the symmetrical position not only of a "child" but also of a "woman", where the "womb" (hysteria) is becoming a part of him and threatens his mental integrity. Lear begs his daughters "do not make me mad" and declares that he is only one step away from using the "woman's weapons, water drops." That is, the symmetry turns Lear into a crying woman whose only weapon is tears. This symmetry threatens Lear, who declares, "No, I'll not weep," but his alternative is flight, both a physical flight from the castle and a mental flight from sanity into madness. Interestingly, becoming mad seems to Lear a better alternative than weeping:

> but this heart
> Shall break into a hundred thousand flaws [i.e., pieces],
> Or ere [i.e., before] I'll weep. O Fool, I shall go mad!

Why does madness seem to be a better option than crying? From the modern perspective, it would seem that Lear cannot express his feelings. However, for Lear, "weeping" is acknowledging the symmetry that turned his life upside down—the symmetry between a man and a woman and a baby and an adult. Crying is the only move possible for the helpless baby, and placing himself in this position, where he knows he cannot trust those who are supposed to care for him, is for Lear a disastrous understanding. From Shakespeare, we also learn an important lesson about personality and symmetry. Living systems always maintain a delicate balance between symmetry and asymmetry and the same holds for human personality. For Lear (who is in a deep conflict), one is either an omnipotent king or a helpless baby, a powerful man or a crying woman. When his omnipotent position cannot be maintained, his default is to fall into the mirror world of helplessness and despair.

THE MADNESS OF KING LEAR

At the beginning of Act 3, Lear is on a heath during an awful storm. He behaves like a mad man when approaching the storm, saying, "Blow winds, and crack your cheeks!" He approaches inanimate physical entities—the winds—as if they were human beings and his enemies. It is a combination of a flight from reality and the projection of his aggression toward nature. Lear, however, acknowledges his desperate state:

> Here I stand your slave—
> A poor, infirm, weak and despised old man.

This is an emotionally moving statement made by a king who has lost his position and turned from a king into what he describes as a slave. However, it is the Fool's response of a specific interpretation and interest:

> He that has a house to put's head in, has a good headpiece.
> The codpiece [penis] that will house [engage in sex]
> Before that head has any [any housing/lodging],
> The head and he shall louse [be infested with lice].

The Fool's comment is interesting because he is describing Lear in sexual terms as a man who follows his sexual urges rather than his reason. The drive motivating the king has blinded him in the same way as a powerful sexual drive may blind a person. The Fool argues that the drive for status and superiority may be no less powerful than the sexual drive. In this sense, the Fool is challenging the Freudian motivational system by emphasizing the importance of the social aspect: the king's narcissistic drive to be superior and the accompanying fear of losing status.

While Lear is portrayed as a typical madman, he recurrently produces statements that indicate his awareness of his situation. For instance, he says,

> When the mind's free,
> The body's delicate. The tempest in my mind
> Doth from my senses take all feeling else.

In other words, he acknowledges the fact that his psychosomatic symptoms and "madness" are the direct result of his "captive" mind and his poisonous thoughts. Lear's madness can be observed in light of another madness, the one played by Edgar.

When Lear's party enters a cabin to seek shelter from the storm, they meet Edgar, who has run away from his father and brother, disguised as a madman. Lear's form of madness is a flight response from the painful reality of the threat to his status. Edgar's form of madness is a practical way of escaping his murderous brother and his raging father. When Lear encounters Edgar's madness, he asks Edgar whether he has arrived at this condition as a result of giving "all to thy daughters." Madness for Lear can result from his own pain alone—a narcissistic and self-centered perspective that sees human suffering from the perspective of one's own.

Edgar's response is "Who gives anything to poor Tom?" His act of mirroring reflects to the king that there are people who have nothing and that their source of suffering is not the loss of everything but the gain of nothing. This reflection is thought provoking as it suggests that Lear, who has lost everything, actually has actually lost himself. As his self is identified with the grandiosity of his status, losing his status is losing everything. The Fool has his own reflection on what a madman is: "He's mad that *trusts* in the tameness of a wolf, a horse's health, a boy's love, or a whore's oath." A madman, according to the Fool, is someone who does not understand real-world constraints, not someone who has lost his status or property. A madman is someone who has unrealistic expectations of reality. A madman is someone who stands behind a horse failing to understand that the horse might kick him and who seeks the oath of a prostitute, who cannot be faithful to a single man. *The madman is therefore someone who cannot accept reality, whether the social reality, the natural reality, or the psychological reality (such as his own pain).*

It is rare to find people who seriously rebel against the natural law of gravity and who torture themselves for not being able to detach from the ground. However, we meet too many people who cannot accept analogue constraints in other domains. For instance, a psychologist once told me about one of her patients who was tortured by the idea that he was too short (170 cm) and therefore could not be attractive to women. As a "short" guy myself, I wondered whether by rebelling against his height, this guy was not performing the same act as rebelling against gravity. Being of a certain height is reality. Being "short" is a judgment with various possible interpretations and implications. The lesson taught by the Fool is that madness is first and foremost a cognitive emotional stance of being unable to accept reality—and, let me add, of paradoxically being unable to accept at the same time that what we call "reality" is to a large extent an illusion. The reality of being "short" is empty in the same way as the reality of being a king is empty. Madness is not about one's genes or one's behavior but about one's distorted understanding of what is there.

This explanation of madness reminds me of a wonderful text in the *Midrash*, which is a body of exegesis of Torah texts along with homiletic stories as taught by the Jewish sages. The specific text of the *Midrash* deals with the festival of Purim, which lauds the Jewish people's survival of the evil plan of the Persian Minister Haman to exterminate the Jews thousands of years ago. (In an interesting coincidence, while I am writing this chapter, Israeli Prime Minister Benjamin Netanyahu is giving a speech to the American Congress in an attempt to stop the Iranian/Persian nuclear plan.) The *Midrash*'s interpretation of the biblical story of Haman's attempt to exterminate the Jews has something interesting to say about Haman and his evil:

> What is an apt parable for Haman the Evil One? To what can he be compared? To a bird which made its nest on the shore of the sea, then the sea came and swept away the nest. The bird said: I will not budge from here until the sea becomes dry land, and the dry land becomes the sea. What did the bird do? It took some water from the sea in its mouth and dropped it on dry land, and took dirt from the land and dropped it into the sea. Its friend came and stood

alongside. He said to the bird: You ill-fated, hapless one! How do you ever hope to succeed?

Midrash, Esther Rabbah 7:10 (Freedman & Simon, 1939)

Observing the bird's behavior, Lear's Fool would not hesitate to diagnose it as mad. It is a narcissistic bird with delusions of omnipotence and responds to the "sea's behavior" with a burst of narcissist range that attempts to annihilate (i.e., dry) the sea. The bird is not ready to accept the simple logic of reality and its behavior is a desperate attempt to fight against it. If madness is a form of a flight response, we can describe it as the ultimate form of flight from acknowledging reality.

Lear is blind to him and to his environment in the same way as Gloucester is blind to Edmund's treason. Symbolically, Gloucester loses his sight when his eyes are plucked out by Cornwall and Regan after they find out that he helped Lear to escape and after Edmund incriminates him as a traitor. The moment when Gloucester loses his physical sight is the moment when Edmund is revealed to him as the person who betrayed him. From a psychological blindness, he moves to physical blindness but gains the understanding that "Edgar was abused." Edgar naivety is challenged when he meets his blind father on the heath (Act 4 Scene 1). By observing his poor father, Edgar realizes the importance of defense mechanisms and psychological distortions:

> But [except] that thy strange mutations [changes] make us hate thee,
> Life would not yield to age [old age].

That is, Edgar realizes that, if we had been able to be omniscient and were able to see the vicissitudes of life, we would probably not have survived or, more accurately, our sanity would not have survived. Being omniscient is accompanied by the horrified realization of what we might encounter in our life. As suggested by the mad king,

> When we are born, we cry that we are come
> To this great stage of fools

Indeed, we come to life with a cry, anticipating "a stage of fools." Edgar also realizes that

> The worst is not
> So long as we can say "This is the worst"

which means that our ability to observe a situation from the outside is crucial to enable us to cope with it. This is an important psychological observation and is evident in the "mindfulness" approach to psychotherapy. Gloucester's response to his situation is less adaptive:

> Our means secure us [money makes us careless], and our mere
>   [absolute] defects
> Prove our commodities

which means that it is better to have less. His way of interpreting the human situation is clearly *depressive*. Man is a "worm"—albeit a conscious worm, as the philosopher Blaise Pascal would have commented—and human beings are to the gods as "flies are to wanton boys," who kill them for sport. In such a painful world, madness and depression are ways of coping by detaching our thoughts from the emotional experience. As suggested by Gloucester:

> Better I were distract [mentally scattered like Lear]
> So should my thoughts be severed from my griefs,
> And woes by wrong imaginations lose

However, as Gloucester cannot "mad" himself by will, he is expressing depression (i.e., a flight response) that leads him to a suicidal plan in which he asks Edgar to bring him to the edge of the cliff, where, through his death, he may "repair [mend] the misery." Edgar's style of coping with the vicissitudes of life is totally different from the coping styles of his father and Lear. The issue of coping with life's misery also occupies Cordelia when she observes her mad father and asks,

> What can man's wisdom [is human wisdom is capable of]
> In the restoring his bereaved [stolen] sense?

Edgar's indirect answer (spoken elsewhere in the play) would have been

> The worst is not
> So long as we can say "This is the worst."

However, both Gloucester and Lear are the prisoners of their own perspectives. When the blind Gloucester and the mad king meet near Dover, Gloucester is excited and asks to kiss the king's hand. Lear's response is "Let me wipe it first, it smells of mortality." Indeed, the hand of a human being "smells of mortality." But what is "dirty" about being mortal? Does immortality suppose to smell like a perfume? This statement indicates Lear's blindness to his human limitations, which is indicative of the *Übermensch*'s pathological thinking. As suggested by Jacques Lacan (cited in Žižek, 2006), the madman is not only the beggar who considers himself to be a king but also the king who considers himself a king. Lear's narcissism is such that he

has lost any perspective on himself as anything other than an *Übermensch.*
The narcissist can never say "this is the worst" as his grandiosity is *infinite*
and, therefore, there is always one more floor to reach before hitting the
ground.

Meanwhile, other people are being disillusioned. The Duke of Albany,
Goneril's husband, realizes the wrong done by his wife to her father. Facing
the invading French army, he refuses to take active steps. Goneril's response
exposes her character:

> It is the cowish [cowardly] terror of his spirit
> That dares not undertake.

Moreover, she says,

> I must change arms at home [be the man of the house] and give the
>   distaff [tool used in spinning; a woman's tool]
> Into my husband's hands.

Goneril lacks empathy. She describes her husband as a coward and, in the
same way as she transformed her father into a baby, transforms her husband
into a woman by proposing to take his manly place. As we can see, symmetry
in the play is associated with disaster. When personality is considered in symmetrical terms, there is always the danger of flipping from one extreme to the
other. Goneril gives her grace to Edmund—the rising star—and promises him
that he will win her and replace her "Milk-livered [cowardly] man."

At this point, Goneril suspects an emerging threat from her sister Regan,
who might compete with her for Edmund's heart. In the final act, the tension reaches its climax. First, the envy between Regan and Goneril in their
competition for Edmund's heart reaches a peak in the form of overt sexual
conflict. Regan asks Edmund whether he loves her sister, and Edmund replies
by saying, "In honored [respectful] love." Edmund probably guesses the hidden intention behind Regan's question, which has a clear sexual meaning. His
answer does not satisfy Regan, who asks,

> But have you never found my brother's way [brother-in-law]
> To the forfended [forbidden] place?

In other words, Regan is interested to know whether Edmund has had sex
with her sister! Such an occurrence would be an immediate threat to Regan,
as it might force Edmund to support a potential offspring and oblige him to
marry her sister. The same threat sheds light on Goneril, who asks her sister,

> Mean you to enjoy [sexually] him?

Edmund denies this possibility and manipulates his way in between the two sisters:

> To both of these sisters have I sworn my love
> Each jealous of [furious at] the other.

He is well aware that he is emotionally manipulating the two sisters, and is guided only by his cold calculations. Meanwhile, Cordelia and Lear have been captured. At this point, Cordelia is suddenly aware that

> We are not the first
> Who with best meaning have incurr'd the worst.

Indeed, as an obsessive personality, she had the "best meaning" when she "kindly" rejected her father's narcissistic needs. However, suddenly she realizes that by following her rigid compass, she has actually incurred the worst possible outcome, as does Brutus in *Julius Caesar*. Called to a duel by Edgar, Edmund loses his life, stating that "The wheel is come to full circle." However, the seeds of his bad intentions cause Regan and Goneril to kill each other, and Cordelia is murdered on his order. While dying of sorrow, Lear says,

> Why should a dog, a horse, a rat, have life!
> And thou no breath at all?

Lear's final words suggest that a human being's life takes some precedence over the life of a dog, a horse, or a rat. He should have read the biblical book of Ecclesiastes, which states that "man hath no pre-eminence above a beast; for all is vanity." This statement raises a philosophical question about the meaning of the concept *Imago Dei*, which refers to humankind being created in the shape of God. For us, the theological issue is of less interest than the psychological one. Even at his point of departure from the world, Lear, as a person suffering from a malignant narcissism, is occupied by issues of status—in this case, the status of human beings as superior to animals, which are located lower on the great chain of being. Lear's narcissism is actually a mirror image of his daughters' and Edmund's rebellion against the same hierarchy.

DISCUSSION

What have we learned from this play?

- That which is beyond measure is actually meaningless.
- Flattery is a form of social grooming and is associated with narcissism.
- The narcissist is surprised by trust violations as he adopts an all-or-nothing trust strategy.

Now, let us conclude with some thoughts about narcissism, flattery, and self-love. We have learned that Lear's narcissism concerns a transformation from low to high status and the need to maintain this high status despite the threat that it poses to others who may strive to climb the ladder of social status, such as Edmund (a bastard). The threat to status is real but the king's self-perception as a superman is an imaginary one. When it is symbolically challenged, such as when Cordelia refuses to serve as Lear's magnifying looking glass, the response is aggressive, of "getting even" by devaluating the person who has challenged the king and reduced his value/meaning. In a deep sense, establishing a sense of self-value is evolutionary and developmentally grounded in our ability to internalize substitutes of caring functions, the same as those used by the mother cat described above. Pathological (i.e., maladaptive) narcissism is therefore associated with some defect in internalization—that is, with the symbolic representation of caring functions.

Psychoanalysts have long argued that we are now living in a narcissistic culture in which the individual is placed at the center of his universe. Like kittens, we are ready to internalize substitutes of caring functions, but cultural dynamics may interfere with these processes to form monstrous distortions and outcomes of this process. In the case of ancient kings, these distortions were "naturally" produced. Kings from the pharaohs to Louis XIV have been the ultimate expressions of malignant narcissism: the complete oblivion of the fact that we are all flesh and blood, and the formation of the imaginary self-conception of a god-like persona. That Louis XIV was known as the "Sun King" is just one instance of this grandiosity, as the sun is deeply associated with goodness (see Schreber's hallucinations for another instance; Schreber, 1903/1988). However, these fantasies of grandiosity have existed since antiquity and, in one case, they are even attributed to the first man. The *Midrash* says, "When the Holy One, blessed be He, created the first man, he created him from one end of the universe to the other." This description of the first man suggests that he filled the entire universe with his size. This is a clear fantasy of grandiosity, which seems to have accompanied human beings from their first appearance on this planet.

In contrast with pathological narcissism, self-love can have a moderate and healthy form that is always aware that the madman is not only the beggar who believes that he is a king but also the king who believes that he is a king. The king who believes that he is a king confuses his grandiose status with his actual existence as a human being who is but a temporary resident in this world, with all the uncertainty, weakness, and fragility that accompany his social and existential status. This healthy realization is perhaps better learned from cats than from human beings. Loving others should not involve seeking our narcissistic reflection in them but rather acknowledging our temporality in them and their temporality within us. If King Lear had been introduced to the mother cat, he may have learned an important lesson about love, self-love, and the price of human hubris.

Othello

On Sperm Competition and the Paranoid General

Surprisingly, mainstream personality theories have never developed different personality dimensions for men and women. In this chapter, I show how different conceptions of threat and trust are involved in the formation of gendered personalities. Othello, a courageous black general who has faced the threat of armed enemies, is defeated by the threat of "sperm competition," which constitutes his "paranoid" personality, and jealously murders his innocent young wife. Through Shakespeare, we learn why men and women are different, and that Proverbs is correct in arguing, "He that is slow to anger is better than the mighty; and he that ruleth his spirit than he that taketh a city."

Why is it that, as readers and audience, we find more interest in villains than in more positive characters who can serve as models for ideal moral behavior? Why can we not find satisfaction is observing a play about the life of Mother Teresa, a nun who dedicated her life to supporting the sick and the poor? Why do we find more interest in the character of the Joker in *The Dark Knight* (Thomas, Eoven, & Nolan, 2008) than in the character of Mother Teresa? Christmas songs are sweet and pleasant but cannot be compared to the effect produced by Bach's *St. Matthew Passion*, with its dramatic tension surrounding the crucifixion of the *agnus Dei* by the Roman villains? One possible explanation is that a villain, as a source of *threat*, produces arousal that attracts our attention. An act of mercy is to be honored. However, as a source of aesthetic amusement, it can be used only when a villain is around, exciting the audience with his wrongdoing. We are attracted to the villain as an informative source of threat and we are aesthetically entertained by his appearance as it is both threatening and relieving at the same time. The threat accompanying the villain is clear but when we encounter a villain in a movie or in a play, we realize that—despite the threat—we are actually safe. The tension has pleasantly faded away. As Freud taught us, pleasure results from the release of tension, and the pleasure of observing a villain in a movie is probably the same as that of observing a roaring lion from within the protective shield of a safari Jeep.

As a talented writer, Shakespeare knew how to create the best villains in town, and one of them, who competes for the title of the master villain of Shakespeare's plays, is Iago, who is probably more of a prominent character in *Othello* than Othello himself. Iago is Othello's ensign, and the play opens with Iago bitterly complaining to Rodrigo, his friend, about the discrimination he has allegedly suffered. Iago knows his "price" but has not received the promotion (and appreciation) that he has asked for from his boss—Othello, a black general, whom Iago describes as "the Moor." If someone is telling us that he knows his value (probably a very high value) and that someone else does not appreciate it, we can immediately hypothesize that we are dealing with a narcissist.

Up to now, nothing seems too bothersome or outrageous. The guy asked for a promotion and did not get it, and he admits that "We cannot all be masters." This seems to be a mature attitude that involves an acceptance that not all of us can be ranked at the top of the social strata. We quickly find out, though, that Iago's "mature" attitude is nothing more than rhetorical lip service to the social norms and that he is actually a person who cannot accept the *narcissistic injury* that he has just suffered from "the Moor." As he admits, "I am not what I am," and his mask of loyal service actually hides vengeful intentions.

Iago's statement puzzles the interpreters of Shakespeare as he does not say "I am not what you see" but rather "I am not what I am." This is an interesting and cryptic *ontological* statement. Ontology is the field of philosophy that deals with what there is: Is there a God? Is there essence underlying the variety of phenomena? And so on.

What does it mean that "I am not what I am"? Let us assume instead that Iago said, "I am what I am." This statement is *tautological*—it is a self-evident statement—and as such it has no informative value. How can one be something different from what one is? However, the statement "I am not what I am" is more puzzling because how can it be that one is not what one is? This statement sounds like a logical contradiction. For now, we will keep this puzzle unresolved; we will return to it later with the assistance of Iago's (imagined) mother and the writings of Bakhtin.

Regardless of the puzzle presented above, at this point, we can strengthen our hypothesis that Iago is a narcissist, and a vengeful one. As we have learned, to the narcissist, the major source of threat is threat to status. When Iago does not get the promotion, he has asked for his "price" or value, which he so proudly extols, he is revealed to be a no more than a balloon full of hot air. The reason is that a person who really acknowledges his "value" does not need the confirmation of others. We all need the confirmation of others but building our sense of self-value based on the confirmation of others is a risky move. In fact, the basic idea of "value" seems to be inherently wrong. Is there a "value" to a human being? Or a sense of value? In talking about "value," we are actually talking about the symbolic substitutes of self-love as have been originally reflected to us through others. Those whose sense of value is sharply influenced by others are people who have a shaky self and are extremely sensitive to status issues.

At this point, we may better elaborate Iago's vengeful intentions. "Getting even" is a phrase that describes the act of revenge. Getting even assumes that there is a system of values one can use for "getting even." How can we get "even" when we do not have a symbolic system that tells us what is equal to what? We have no agreed meter to enable us to determine a "measure for measure," to use the title of one of the Shakespeare's plays—nothing to determine the price one should pay for insulting a narcissist. In this context, the revenge planned by Iago is of great diagnostic value as our system of values deeply reflects our personality. Let us return to the plot.

Othello is married to the young and beautiful Desdemona and, under the orders of Iago, Rodrigo hurries to "poison" Brabantio, her father. Waking the poor father from his sleep, they poison his mind by telling him that an old black "ram" is coupling with his "white [innocent] ewe" and that this "devil" might turn him into a grandfather. The poison prepared by Iago is composed of basic ingredients that exist in every racist's kitchen. The ingredients seem as if they were taken from *Django Unchained* (Sher, Hudin, & Savone, 2012), a provocative film directed by Quentin Tarantino that brutally exposes racism against black people and the fantasies of revenge experienced by the victims. The idea of a "nigger" coupling with an "innocent" white woman is scandalous to a racist's mind. However, in *Othello*, the woman with "whiter skin . . . than snow" having interracial sex with the "black ram" is not an anonymous white woman but Brabantio's own daughter, who might have a child from this breeding "devil." At this point, Richard Dawkins' theory of the selfish gene may pop into the reader's mind. We can try to explain Brabantio's anxiety in terms of his unconscious hardwired wish that the genes of his own group will be propagated. This is, of course, a shaky, reductionist explanation, as from a genetic perspective, there is full justification for "mixing" the genes of different "races."

The same sexual threat returns later, when Othello is described as a "Barbary horse" and a "lascivious Moor" who uses his "gross clasps" (i.e., monstrous embrace) to have sex with the young lady. By inciting Brabantio against Othello, Iago plans to get even by taking Othello's own love—Desdemona.

Here we can start to understand Iago's system of values and the way it reflects his narcissistic persona and vengeful intentions.

For Iago, *the loss of status*, for which he aims to get even, *is equal to the loss of love*. Love equals status. This system of equivalence is strikingly diagnostic of the narcissistic personality as, for the narcissist, status (which is his rank in a group) is equal to love. This is an additional "semiotic" layer of understanding that we may add to the narcissistic character. Without his status, which involves the devaluation of some and the idealization of others, the narcissist does not feel beloved. This is precisely the same dynamic that we observed in analyzing *King Lear*. Whether we are beggars or kings, rich or poor, beautiful or ugly, Nobel laureates or unnoticed academics, we all deserve the love that should have originally come from our caregivers.

Othello teaches us an important lesson about the narcissistic personality and about the narcissistic culture in which some of us live, which *equalizes love with status*. The play points to the mistake of the narcissist who equates status with love and to the price that one might pay for this form of being-in-the-world. Unconditional love is likely something that Iago never experienced as a child; his value was probably determined by his imagined rank. After all, what kind of a status does a baby have except for the rank imagined, mirrored, and projected by his caregivers? There is another way to think about the formation of self-love, which is grounded both in our mother cat example in the previous chapter and in the sophisticated epistemology of Bakhtin. As beautifully written by Bakhtin (1990, p. 23),

> As we gaze at each other, two different worlds are reflected in the pupils of our eyes. . . . This ever-present *excess* of my seeing, knowing, and possessing in relation to any other human being is founded in the uniqueness and irreplaceability of my place in the world.

This is a profound insight. As we gaze at each other, *two different* worlds are reflected, not my projected world as reflected from you or vice versa. Individuality, at least according to Bakhtin, is built into each and every one of us, and we all have a unique and irreplaceable perspective on the world. Therefore, my value is primarily determined by my uniqueness as a human being who has a specific perspective on this world and not by the projected grandiosity of a narcissistic mother observing her child in admiration as reflecting her own fantasies.

The uniqueness of my perspective on the world has value only in a system of exchange, in which this form of uniqueness can be acknowledged. Practically speaking, our uniqueness and value in the world are based on the recognition of others, and in fact on the *mutual recognition* of others. Now we are in a position to better understand the developmental aspect of malignant narcissism. For example, we may imagine Iago's mother—let us call her Yaga[1]—interacting with her young toddler and saying to him:

> Oh Iago, my son, one day you will be a great man, so great that you will deserve my love, as love my son is about *what* you will be and not about *who* you are.

Having imagined this dialogue between Iago and his mother, I would like to take a break in the flow of this chapter and to drift away to clarify the difference between "what you are" and "who you are." Let me just warn the reader that at this point, we are entering a discussion that is highly abstract and philosophical.

"LIFT YOUR EYES ON HIGH": WHAT IS THE DIFFERENCE BETWEEN "WHAT" AND "WHO" YOU ARE?

Rabbi Shlomo Carlebach (1925–1994), known as the "Singing Rabbi," was a hippy rabbi who was also a Jewish musician, teacher, and singer. In one of his lessons (undated), Carlebach said that there are two questions one may ask oneself. The first is "*What* are you?" and the second is "*Who* are you?" Carlebach associated the first question with a negative valence and the second with a positive valence. His teaching is a free improvisation on *The Zohar*, the most important Jewish mystical text. *The Zohar* says,

> Who created this (Isaiah, 40:26) . . . *Lift your eyes on high* . . . There you will discover that the concealed ancient one, susceptible to questioning, *created these*. Who is that? *Who*. (1:1b)

In footnote 27, the commentary explains that "The mystical name *Who* becomes a focus of meditation, as question turns into quest." In contrast with the "Who," "there is another below called *What*" (1:1b):

> What distinguishes the two? The first concealed one—called *Who*—can be questioned. Once a human being questions and searches, contemplating and knowing rung after rung to the very last rung—once one reaches there: *What?* What do you know? What have you contemplated? For what have you searched? All is concealed as before. (Matt, 2004, 1:1b).

Carlebach's reading of *The Zohar* takes the above questions originally addressed to God and turns them inward as psychological questions addressed to the human being. What is the difference between the questions "What are you?" and "Who are you?"

The first—"What are you?"—is a question of *reification*. It is a question that invites an answer in terms of an *object* or, more accurately, in terms of a general category: "I am X." For instance, when asked "What are you?" Lear could have easily respond by saying "I am THE king." This answer grasps only a superficial aspect of a human being. The second question—"Who are you?"—is a "question turned into a quest." It is not a question leading to an answer but a question that opens an inquiry that cannot be answered simply by stipulating an abstract category of language: "I am X."

As long as we ask the "what" question, the tragedy of reification is inevitable. Answering the "what" question entails objectifying people by putting them into small boxes that they might mistakenly identify with the answer to the "who" question. The king who conceives himself a king is just one instance of this pathological dynamic. This tragedy of reification has been discussed by Bakhtin as the tragedy of "theorization" and it is insightfully elaborated in his earliest major work and one of his less-known essays, "Toward a Philosophy of the Act" (Bakhtin, 1999; originally published around 1919).

In this essay, Bakhtin's opening sentence declares that "aesthetic activity [i.e., theorization] . . . is powerless to take possession of that moment of Being which is constituted by the transitiveness and open event-ness of Being" (Bakhtin, 1999, p. 1) and hence "aesthetic contemplation as well is unable to grasp once-occurrent Being-as-event in its singularity" (p. 14). In other words, theorization is an act of partitioning the world, whether the internal or the external, into static categories through the symbolic and abstract power of language. As such it is unable to grasp its object of inquiry as a dynamic object. This criticism can clearly be applied to personality theory, where the use of a few personality types is "powerless" in representing the "transitiveness" and "open event-ness" of real human beings. According to Bakhtin, this theorization is justified only as long as it does not go beyond its own boundaries, which means that it is perfectly legitimate to theorize as long as we acknowledge the limits of theorization. However, when theorization arrogantly pretends to see "once-occurrent Being-as-event in its singularity," it is "doomed to passing off an *abstractly isolated part* as the actual whole" (p. 17, emphasis mine). Therefore, "all attempts to force one's way from inside the theoretical world into actual 'Being-as-event' are quite hopeless" (p. 12), which means that *there is an unbridgeable gap between the world and our simple and abstract representation of the world*, between our schemes and the actual complex and wild dynamics of real life and real people. The only place where this gap is seriously encountered is in *literature*, and specifically the novel, which can somehow represent "Being-as-event" in a way no other medium can do (Kundera, 1988). Here we can add another layer to our understanding of how important literature is in bridging the gap between the limited abstract theorization and "Being-as-event."

The task of bridging the gap between our theorization and the real and messy world is utopian and we must always struggle to maintain it. There is no transcendental or *a priori* justification for our theorization and, in this sense, there is no "alibi" in existence, either in our interpretation of ourselves or our interpretation of others. This is not a simple idea and I would like to further develop it.

The idea of no alibi is a cornerstone of Bakhtin's attempt to address the symbolic gap between the world and our representation of the world. In this context, he argues that I have "no alibi" in this world because I cannot claim to have been elsewhere than in the concrete and actual place where a deed is performed. I cannot observe my existence from an abstract perspective as if I were God, or from a theoretical perspective as if I were observing an object. *The narcissist who feels god-like may try to adopt such a perspective in which he is beyond Being-as-event.* This is precisely the cognitive distortion of the king who believes he is a king and refuses to accept the fact that there is no alibi in existence and that his "royal" perspective is temporary, limited, and uncertain—the same as that of any other human being.

According to Bakhtin, I can fully observe life only from my own particular and singular place where a deed is performed. Bakhtin suggests that I am not an object naturally given, such as a stone or a drop of water, but an active and morally responsible human being who is constantly aware of *the gap between the self and the representation of the self* and must operate in the world through this gap. Therefore, my "no alibi" is a hole in the fabric of our existence, which Bakhtin considered as crucial for authentically living (rather than bridging) the gap between the world and the representation of the world. Indeed, if you are a talented intelligence agent who strives to understand human beings, you are probably not occupied with bridging the gap between your academic psychological schemes and real people, but with *living* the gap and *operating* in it.

This gap, described as a hole in the fabric of reality, may turn into a loophole through which one may escape the tragedy of "becoming-as-such"—of becoming an object among objects. This loophole is *acknowledging*, which can save us from being no more than a "natural given" (Bakhtin, 1990, p. 40). In other words, the fact that I (and other human beings) have a unique perspective on the world that cannot be grasped through abstract theorization is precisely what saves me from being an object, in the same way as it saves others from being caricatures of abstract psychological schemes. This loophole is a point of noncoincidence between me and my representation of other people, and through it I may change myself. It is a process of reflection through which my perspective, which does not converge with those of other people, gives me a better perspective from which I may observe the "who" question.

Where does the point of noncoincidence exist? Bakhtin answers this question by suggesting that the loophole exists at the meeting point between me and the other. It is the meeting point where I can save myself from the schemes in which I am caged. The "loophole" evident in the nonconverging perspectives of human beings destabilizes my own rigid conception of my self. Through the two different worlds reflected in our pupils, we challenge our image through the other's gaze: *I am not what you think I am!*

We have now introduced some of Bakhtin's sophisticated ideas and it is time to return to the play and to attempting to explain the persona of Iago. When Iago says "I am not what I am," he is actually denying his unique position in the world and the idea that there is no alibi in existence. Iago's alibi is in "I am not what I am" and "you are what you are." For example, to him the "Moor" is a devil full of lust. Othello is far from being a devil full of lust, but from Iago's perspective, "you are what you are," an object reified through the observer's gaze, an answer to the "what" question. We can ask Iago from which theoretical position such a distorted conception of Othello is justified. There is no such theoretical perspective but only Iago's own distortions, for which he is responsible. However, when he says "I am not what I am," he is seeking an alibi. While Iago distances himself from his position as a moral agent, his conception of others is asymmetrically fixed and rigid; Othello is a devilish Moor, women are whores, and so on.

The loophole described by Bakhtin exists at the place where our unique perspectives are reflected by each other. Like two mirrors facing each other, what we get is not a simple representation of my-self or the other-self, not an answer to the "what" question, but a mystery constituted by the mutual gaze and the two incommensurable horizons. A hero who illustrates this fascinating dynamic appears a short story: "The Twenty-Seventh Man," by Nathan Englander. The reading of this short story is another point where the complexity of our interpretation reaches a peak.

"THE TWENTY-SEVENTH MAN"

"The Twenty-Seventh Man" is a short story that appears in Englander's celebrated book *For the Relief of Unbearable Urges* (1999). The story is about 27 Yiddish writers who have been arrested and are awaiting execution during the dark days of Stalin's regime. The 27th person was not originally included in the list. His name is Pinchas Pelovitz and he is described as a young man who has built his world on the idea of a compassionate God and who tests people with moral dilemmas and tragedies.

As we can see, Pelovitz uses literature as a laboratory in a similar way to the idea proposed in the preface of this book. However, Pelovitz never published his stories and it is clear that he has been included in the celebrated list of Yiddish writers by mistake. The question "What are you, Pinchas Pelovitz?" (a Yiddish writer?) cannot be simply answered as he is not *really* a writer but has been arrested and jailed as such. Stalin's agents ignored the more complex "who" question and were probably satisfied with the "what" question, which includes Pelovitz as an answer, though by mistake.

Having been arrested, Pelovitz is severely beaten by Stalin's agents and taken to prison, where he refuses to acknowledge that his arrest is a bureaucratic mistake. His response to the tragic situation in which his humanity is taken from him and he is treated like an object is a deed: *writing his final story*. Therefore, we have a story within a story and, as will be finally seen, a *loophole* story illustrating the unique liberating power of literature through the loophole perspective.

The story written by Pelovitz is about a person by the name of Mendel Muskatev, who awakes one day to find that "his desk was gone, his room was gone, and the sun was gone" (Englander, 1999, p. 21). This is, of course, a metaphor for Pelovitz's own life facing a dead end. Muskatev's understanding of the situation is that he has passed away. The reader's corollary is that the world has "died" too, as a world in which the "sun was gone" is a world that has reached its end. What would you imagine your reaction to be upon finding that the world as you have known it has reached its end? In my mind arise apocalyptic novels such as Cormac McCarthy's *The Road* (2006). These are thrilling novels that powerfully express the inevitable *horror* one may experience in the face of such a catastrophe. Surprisingly, and like his author (Pelovitz), Muskatev responds to the bizarre situation with a deed: reciting the Jewish prayer for the dead (the *Kaddish*). That is, instead of responding with horror and agony, Muskatev seems quite indifferent to the situation, albeit he follows the Jewish law and custom obliging him to say a specific prayer for the dead. Muskatev's indifference is reminiscent of the hero of another story, "The Metamorphosis," by Franz Kafka (2012). In the story, Gregor Samsa wakes one day to find that he has been transformed into a cockroach, and attempts to keep on living as if nothing happened.

In the story within "The Twenty-Seventh Man," instead of responding to the situation with anxiety, Muskatev is worried by another issue, which is the appropriateness of his deed and whether he is allowed, according to the Jewish law, to say the prayer for himself. That is, Muskatev is aware that he is dead, but his outside perspective—through the loophole, one may say—gives him an opportunity to practice the Jewish law. He sets off to consult the local rabbi and is surprised to find that the rabbi's study is the same as his own missing room. The rabbi is therefore an imaginary twin of Muskatev and occupies the same mental space. When Muskatev communicates his conclusion to the rabbi, that they are both dead, the rabbi's surprising response is a kind of joy, thanking Muskatev for noticing that he is in heaven and that he is now free to study the Talmud. Hurrying to study the Talmud with passion and joy, the rabbi asks Muskatev whether there is another reason for his visit. Muskatev's response is emotionally moving, as something breaks inside his stoic response: " 'I wanted to know'—and here his voice began to quiver— 'which one of us is to say the prayer [for the dead].' "

Being trapped by the invasion of chaos into his life, Muskatev does not seek meaning outside the frame in which he finds himself but instead seeks to determine the appropriate deed through the loophole perspective. For Muskatev, there is no alibi in existence and no alibi in death too. Instead of theorizing or reflecting on his death from an abstract perspective, he chooses to act and to do the right thing. The only loophole through which Muskatev may experience himself as a singularity, as a person worth living his life and experiencing his death as a nonobject, is therefore his noncoincident gaze with his imaginary twin—the rabbi. The rabbi's joy is noncoincident with Muskatev's anxiety, although the two occupy the same imaginary space. The intersection of these noncoincident gazes of Muskatev and his imaginary twin is precisely the place where the deed should take place. The deed is the only possible response to the invasion of the chaos and the recognition that, unlike other objects that have been annihilated from the world (i.e., the sun, the table), Muskatev's death is the death of a unique individual created in God's image, an individual whose disappearance from this world should be acknowledged with a ritual: the *Kaddish*. This is the end of the story, and the author, Pelovitz, is praised for it by his cellmates a moment before their execution. A moment before the anxiety of death riches its climax and the prisoners are executed, Pelovitz is warmly embraced by his caring mates, which turns his final story into a meaningful deed. The story is a loophole, in which the hero is the author of a story in which the hero finds the meaning of his encounter with the painful reality through the appropriate deed and through the authentic empathy of his noncoincident twins: the "true" Yiddish writers in the story and the rabbi within Muskatev's story.

If we are to look for the meaning of Pelovitz's personal tragedy, the ultimate explanation is that a clerk has made a mistake. This interpretation is unacceptable as it leaves Pelovitz naked in the face of chaos as an object "in and for itself," to use an expression coined by Edmund Husserl. However, this meaning should be suspended until the last minute and then replaced by a interpretation that is introduced to the plot via a story within the story. The answer to the question "What are you, Pinchas Pelovitz?" (a Yiddish writer who is doomed to death because of what he is) should be suspended until the "who" question can be introduced, and the "who" question, as previously argued, is the one that opens a loophole rather than closing the plot. As *The Zohar* teaches, "*Who* becomes a focus of meditation, as question turns into quest."

The kabbalistic teaching challenges us to consider an alternative to the narcissistic perspective of Iago. Instead of asking the "what" question, we should ask the "who" question. Asking "who" saves us not only from the simple representational view rejected by postmodernism and poststructuralism but also from the annihilation of the individual. According to the perspective presented here, the individual and his unique place in the world are secured through his noncoincident gaze with the other. Such a form of individuality emphasized by the Talmudic scholars does not involve a naive conception of the "self" sometimes criticized by poststructuralism. It is individuality constituted through loopholes, a process in which the individual constantly and reflectively struggles to avoid his reification by himself and by others. This perspective is missing from Iago's life and the consequences are disastrous.

"I NEVER FOUND A MAN THAT KNEW HOW TO LOVE HIMSELF"

As cited above, Iago admits that he is not familiar with self-love. Self-love is what Freud described as healthy narcissism. Healthy self-love is modeled after the love of our caregivers; we love ourselves in the same way as we have been loved by those who raised us and taught us to gain trust in this world. In a case where self-love, or healthy narcissism, is developmentally defective, we may hypothesize that healthy parental love was missing and that pathological narcissism emerged as a defensive facade. This pathological narcissism is evident when *status turns into a substitute for love*. In fact, Iago's concept of love is far from the caring form of love even when it concerns the love between a man and a woman. For example, Roderigo, his friend, is deeply in love with Desdemona, but Iago dismisses this feeling, saying that love is a specific expression of "carnal" irritations and unrestrained "lusts." How far is this limited conception of love from caring and romantic love? Given the knowledge you have gained so far, how would you imagine Iago's attitude toward women in general? Cassio (Othello's lieutenant) welcomes Iago, his wife Emilia, and Desdemona when they arrive in Cyprus. As an act of politeness, Cassio kisses Emilia. Iago's response is cynical:

> Sir, would she give you so much of her lips
> As of her tongue she oft bestows [confers] on me,
> You'll have enough.

This cynical and vicious comment initiates a "Who's afraid of Virginia Woolf" kind of trialogue between Iago, Emilia, and Desdemona. This situation exposes Iago's chauvinistic opinions. He describes women as "wild cats," noisemakers, saints and devils, and "housewives" (i.e., hussies) in bed. These descriptive tags and others expose a highly negative and compartmentalized concept of women. A woman, whether his wife or another, is not conceived by Iago as a complex yet integrated being, but as a split object: a saint and a devil, someone who can never be trusted. But what do you expect from someone who lacks self-love?

Iago's narcissism is also evident in omnipotent statements such as "Our bodied are our gardens, to the which our wills are gardeners." The idea that our wills can control our bodies in such a simple and arrogant manner is an omnipotent fantasy. The older we get, the more we (are supposed to) understand how limited we are in controlling our body. The idea that our body is a garden that is submissive to the will of a gardener is refuted upon our first encounter with pain. Indeed, pain is the ultimate test of the reality principle. Taking LSD and believing that one is a dolphin jumping over the tranquil waves of the ocean may be a convincing illusion until one hits the ground when jumping from the third floor.

When Brabantio finally approaches Othello, he blames him for stealing his daughter. He cannot even imagine the possibility that his white and gentle daughter fell in love with the Moor and blames Othello for "enchanting" her, using "drugs" and "chains of magic." The Moor, as an earthly incarnation of the devil, is suspected of using supernatural forces and dirty tricks, as if a woman cannot naturally fall in love with such a man. However, Desdemona confesses her love and marriage to the Moor, putting an end to the dispute. However, the bitter father refuses to emotionally accept this situation. This scene plays out in front of the Duke, and the Duke tries to psychologically support the father by saying,

> To mourn a mischief that is past and gone
> Is the next way to draw new mischief on.

That is, the Duke, who appreciates both Brabantio and Othello, advises Brabantio to put aside his mourning as rumination over a lost past is in itself a source of misery. This is a wise psychological lesson that Brabantio refuses to accept:

> But words are words; I never yet did hear
> That the bruised heart was pierced through the ear.

In other words, the same person who previously blamed the Moor for using spells and magic is now denying the power of words to heal! If words can do harm through black magic, they can heal too. "Words are words" is a statement that drains the value out of words, as a word that is just a word is devoid of meaning and affect. Some modern psychotherapeutic techniques, such as acceptance and commitment therapy, use precisely this kind of logic when they ask patients to repeat the same word again and again, like a mantra, until it is drained of its threatening content and affect.

Imagine Brabantio attending a psychotherapeutic session in which he expresses his deep agony at finding out that his daughter has married a "Moor."

"But 'Moor,'" explains the psychologist, "is just a word."

"What do you mean?" asks Brabantio. "A word is not just a word! This Moor is black! The dark side of the moon! What can't you understand?"

"Hmm," says the psychologist. "Let's try to do something. Please repeat the word 'Moor' one hundred times."

"Moor, Moor, Moor . . .," repeats Brabantio, until the word loses its devilish connotations and becomes an *empty signifier*. "Well, this is amazing," he says. "I've told the Duke that words are just words!"

Iago keeps saying that he hates the Moor, but why does he express such hate for someone who did not promote him? Later, and in one of his confessions, Iago provides us with a better explanation:

> And it is thought abroad [widely], that' twixt my sheets
> He [Othello] has done my office [sexual role of the husband].

Here we expose Iago's sexual source of racial hate and his suspicion that Othello has had sex with his wife. Later, in another scene, he repeats the same theme:

> For that I do suspect the lusty Moor
> Hath leap into my seat.

This imagined fear is described as a "poisonous mineral" and the planned revenge involves putting the Moor into a "jealousy so strong" that judgment cannot "cure" it. An eye for an eye, a wife for a wife, and jealousy for jealousy. The vengeful mind is a mind that seeks to equate the pain of the avenger with the pain of his victim, as clearly expressed by Iago's monologues. Iago admits that he has no solid ground for this suspicion, but this does not matter. For the narcissist who is not familiar with self-love, the imagined Moor is not a threat to intimate relations and true love but a *threat to status*, a threat that may be conceived as evolutionary grounded in sperm competition too. To recall, sperm competition concerns the competition between several males to fertilize the same female. Sperm competition attempts to explain sexual jealousy and has been found to be a leading cause in partner killing

(Buss, 2006, cited in Pham & Shackelford, 2014). Sexual jealousy is also an expression of a paranoid projection: I am afraid that you will have sex with my females as I have the same intentions with regard to your females. Sexual jealousy is also associated with status, as men compete with each other on the basis of social dominance rather than physical attractiveness per se (Maner & Shackelford, 2008). In other words, if a man sees his spouse giggling with a handsome but poor young surfer, he will likely feel less concerned than upon seeing his spouse giggling with a handsome and young billionaire. Now, think about a movie such as *Indecent Proposal* (Lansing, 1993). In this film, Robert Redford plays a billionaire who proposes to a couple who have lost all of their savings that he will give them one million dollars to have sex with the wife. In this case, we have a competitive male (Robert Redford's character) who is both physically attractive and socially superior. In this context, men may feel deep empathy with the painful feelings of the husband, who agrees to the "indecent proposal."

Given the context of sperm competition, there is a good reason to suspect that Iago would feel threatened by Othello. Othello is a highly appreciated general who has a higher social status than Iago and is probably physically attractive. Othello is also a classic other, similar to Jews accused in Nazi Germany of seducing young Aryan girls. Do you remember Bakhtin and his "As we gaze at each other, two different worlds . . ."? For Bakhtin, the other and his nonconverging perspective is a proof of our *own uniqueness* but for the racist, the other is a threat to his uniqueness. The reason is that, when the narcissist gazes at the other, he expects to see a reflection of his own grandiosity, like the mythological Narcissus. What happens if, instead of our reflected grandiosity, we observe something quite different? To answer this question, let us recall that reflection, such as the mythological Narcissus' reflection in a pool, is actually our way of describing the *mirroring* process through which we have been socialized. The developmental origin of "As we gaze at each other . . ." is the way we have been mirrored by our caregivers. When a narcissist such as Iago gazes at Othello, what he sees is not only a totally differentiated individual who cannot serve as an empowering looking glass but also a differentiated individual who is of a supposedly lower social status albeit actually with a higher social status. Sperm competition would have made Iago highly sensitive to the threat of all males of higher social status who are potential competitors. However, the fact that Iago's jealousy is focused on Othello is an indication that we cannot be satisfied by the evolutionary explanation per se. Sexual jealousy, specifically when it involves racial issues, is of a narcissistic character. Think about the Nazi conflict with Jewish sexuality and its alleged threat to the purity of the Aryan race. Why should the blond, blue-eyed, and well-built Aryan *Übermensch* be threatened by the Jew, who has been described as a subhuman creature?

Simplified to a nutshell of psychological interpretation, the Nazi dynamic is all about status, superiority, and inferiority. As we have learned from modern psychodynamic theory (McWilliams, 2011, 2012), personality is all about zones of preoccupation, and the narcissist's major area of preoccupation is his conflict with status and the threat to status. The Nazis were therefore pathological narcissists who, like Iago, targeted their hate to the ultimate other, who was also of a supposedly lower social status but actually had impressive achievements that threatened the Nazis' own shaky grandiosity.

Extrapolating from the level of individual psychology to the collective consciousness of a group is a tricky undertaking. However, as we have learned from the seminal work of Voloshinov (1929/1986), this extrapolation is not only justified but inevitable, as the source of human psychology is in the social realm, which is reflected and refracted by individual minds. Interestingly, the revenge planned by Iago reflects his major source of threat, and this revenge finds fertile soil in Othello, another narcissist, who in a deep sense is a mirror image of his most bitter enemy.

INTO THE TRAP

Othello the general reminds us in his *naiveté* of another general we have met in Shakespeare's plays: Julius Caesar. Like Caesar, Othello is a narcissist who is defective in his judgment and in managing his trust of others. This point has been identified by Harold Bloom, who describes Othello as "incapable of seeing himself except in grandiose terms" (Shakespeare, 2005, pp. 221–222).

In contrast with Emilia and Desdemona, who are quick to suspect Iago's true nature, Othello's judgment is diametrically opposed to Iago's true nature and he conceives Iago as "most honest." This is the context for Iago's plan, and the plan is simple. After involving the handsome Cassio in an incident that causes Othello to dismiss him, Iago proposes to Cassio to try to regain his position by supplication to Desdemona, as the "general's wife is now the general." Here is another place where a substitute is of psychological significance; the general's wife equals the general. This equation exposes the psycho-logic guiding Iago, which is to hurt the wife for hurting her husband as if they are the same person. Iago forecasts that the good-hearted Desdemona will ask Othello to forgive Cassio, but, Iago says,

> I'll pour this pestilence [mischief] into his [Othello's] ear,
> That she repeals [calls upon him] for her body's lust.

In other words, Iago aims to plant in Othello's mind the suspicion that Desdemona is helping Cassio because she is sexually attracted to him.

Moreover, the plan is to create a situation where Othello will find Cassio soliciting Desdemona:

> And bring him jump when he may Cassio find
> Soliciting his wife. Ay, that's the way.

The whole of this process is done with "soft words." As we may recall from the analysis of *Julius Caesar* and *King Lear*, "soft words" are used by villains to overcome the defenses of their victims. This tactic is consciously acknowledged by Iago, who says,

> When devils will [want to] the blackest sins put on,
> They do suggest [propose] at first with heavenly shows.

The "heavenly shows" of Iago gain Othello's trust and the spider's web begins to come into being. The first seed of suspicion is implanted by Iago when he and Othello enter a room while Cassio is leaving after discussing his bad fortune with Desdemona. Iago's first comment is quite vague: "Ha? I like not that." Othello, who does not understand Iago, asks for clarification, but Iago dismisses this clarification: "Nothing, my lord." This dismissal is a discursive cover to something that should raise the suspicion of Othello, who swallows the bait by asking, "Was not that Cassio parted from my wife?" Iago throws the bait and Othello is quick to catch it. However, bait is only bait when a fish has *a priori* interest in worms. An overdeveloped scheme of suspicion (Beck, 1979) guides Othello's interpretation of Iago's allegedly innocent comment. Othello, therefore, not only is a narcissistic general but also clearly has a paranoid mind that feels deep conflict over trust and fear of threatening others, in this case the imagined threat of his cheating wife.

Iago strengthens Othello's suspicion by saying that he cannot think that Cassio would "steal away so guilty-like." These are soft words in action. First, a cue is sent into the air. Like a Rorschach inkblot, this cue is presented to the victim for interpretation and under the guidance of the villain turns into an image of the victim's main imaginary source of threat and anxiety. As our intelligence agent may learn, vague regions in conversations between people are immediately filled with interpretations that are actually projections indicative of our threat- and trust-management systems.

Othello becomes aware of what Iago is suggesting and asks him whether Cassio is honest. Iago replies, "Honest, my lord!" and thus refrains from answering the question. When asked "What dost thou think?" Iago answers "Think, my lord!" Othello seems to be angry:

> By heaven, he echoes me,
> As if there were some monster in his thought
> Too hideous to be shown.

He is correct, of course, but the monster is Iago's real plan of revenge.

Our intelligence agent also knows that manipulating others involves the ability to use soft words to access their most basic conflicts, unconsciously of course. Resistance to such a kind of manipulation cannot be built on awareness only. The fact that one understands that one is being manipulated by others does not guarantee one's success in resisting the manipulation. To resist a manipulation, one also has to be an individual who has resolved his innermost conflicts.

Othello, despite his courage on the battlefield, despite his status as a successful general, and despite the fact that he is a man loved by a wonderful woman, is a man who is mentally organized around a deep conflict over trust. What we learn is that, regardless of one's success, position, and status, and regardless of admired personality characteristics such as courage, one can be occupied with a conflict that can lead one's life astray. This idea turns our oversimplified psychological understanding upside down, as it points out that the homogenous, coherent, and well-structured concept of personality is ungrounded. By that, I do not mean that the diagnosis of Othello as presented in this chapter is false but just that a possible and naive expectation that a successful and brave general will be conflict-less and immune to manipulation is ungrounded.

Iago uses the paradoxical strategy that we have encountered in interpreting Julius Caesar, a strategy that seems as if it were taken from the school of Milton Erickson. "O, beware my lord, of jealousy" he advises Othello, while paradoxically directing him to suspect the disloyalty of Desdemona. What is the first reason raised by Othello for such a possible disloyalty? The answer is his black color ("Haply for I am black"); the second reason is his lack of those "soft parts of conversation" that gallants have; and the third reason is his age. The first reason is an indication of his narcissistic character. His wife, who chose him regardless of her father's prejudice, may be cheating on him for the same reason her father chose to reject him. It is clear that Othello's explanation is far-fetched because, if Desdemona did not like his color, she could have chosen someone else from the beginning. The fear that his wife is cheating on him because he is black, uncivilized, and old reflects Othello's own conflicts with his color, status, and age—conflicts internalized from the racial hate of some of his social milieu.

The conflict is nurtured by imagination. We have learned that a threat can be real or imagined, and, paradoxically, imagined threats cast a dark spell over some people's souls. Imagined threats are formed despite a lack of rigid evidence. In this context, the mind may complete the picture through its own distorted schemes. It is acknowledged by Othello that

'tis better to be much abused
Than but to know't a little.

The reason is that the incomplete and distorted picture formed by Iago turns Othello's imagination into a wild beast, and a poisoned imagination fuels the tragedy in the same way as it fueled the tragedy of Chekhov's government clerk— Ivan Dmitritch Tchervyakov—who is led astray by his wild imagination. At this point, we may learn something interesting about the *power of doubt*.

It seems that doubt has a much more powerful impact on our minds than certainty. It is as if we are essentially programmed to work with two binary possibilities—know and do not know—and as if a doubt, located in between, may drive us crazy. Why is it so difficult to live with doubt? As I am writing this chapter in 2015, I recall that this week I visited a colleague of mine who has lost her 22-year-old son in the devastating earthquake that took place in Nepal. For 2 weeks, the family and supporting volunteers searched for this young man until they found his body on the edge of a cliff overlooking a river. The mother shared with me her fear that they would never find her son's body. Having realized that their son was no longer among the living, she and her husband desperately wished to bring his body "back home" for a funeral. For them, the idea of living in doubt was torture.

The etymology of "doubt" teaches us that the word originated in the Old French *dote*, meaning "to fear." Indeed, *living in doubt is living in fear*. In contrast with doubt, "certain" is etymologically grounded in the Vulgar Latin *certus*, meaning "fixed," which is a variant of *cernere*, meaning "to separate." Doubt is so difficult to bear because it does not allow us to conceive the world as stable and compartmentalized into "digestible" forms, to draw on the metaphorical phrase used by Wilfred Bion. Living in doubt is living in a situation where we have to handle the turbulences of the Heraclitian river rather than the stability of a tranquil lake. It is a situation where the integrity of our separated identity encounters the thantalic (from Thanatus) force that threatens to annihilate us. Living in doubt is living in a labyrinth. As poetically written by Attali (1999, p. xxiv), "my own life is like a labyrinth, with blind alleys, and about-faces, where I often discover that I am further from the center just when I believe that I have found it." This labyrinthine way of living and thinking is remote from the straight-line kind of reasoning that involves reason and certainty. Living in doubt is like navigating in a dark forest, but, as Attali reminds us, life is more similar to a dark forest than to the artificial invention of the straight line. Therefore, living in doubt is an inevitable part of living life itself. For our intelligence agent, whenever there is doubt, there is a situation that epitomizes life in its living complexity. One who strives for *certus*—fixed—meaning in life may become angry when having to live the fear of doubt. A person who cannot live with doubt as an inherent component of his life should not work as an intelligence agent.

How it is that Othello, a brave general who is not afraid of encountering death on the battlefield, is made mad by doubt? The answer can be found in the narcissistic and paranoid lines of his personality. Previously, and following the etymology of doubt, I described doubt as a thantalic force. In Greek mythology, Thanatos was the demon of nonviolent death and was accompanied by his twin brother, Hypnos (sleep). While Othello seems to bravely face the idea of violent death that accompanies war, he is helpless in encountering the dreamy nature of Thanatus and the Hypnos manipulated by the soft words of Iago.

Indeed, the situation on the battlefield is clear cut: the enemy is obvious. It is a situation of life or death where the threat is real, the response is clear, and the best man will win. However, when the seeds of jealousy and doubt are planted in his mind, Othello has to deal with a much more complex situation in which the nature of the enemy and the rules of the game are far from clear. As a narcissist, and similar to Iago, his alter-ego, Othello lives through his reflected image in the stable pool of life. Throughout the play, the image reflected of Othello from his surrounding social milieu is one of a hero. But what happens when he observes his beautiful image blurs and finds it difficult to see himself under the doubt implanted by Iago? The answer is that the narcissist cannot live without his reflected image as the default is an empty self, terrified of being lost in the dark forest. This interpretation suggests that there is also a strong paranoid dimension in Othello's personality. As a paranoid tortured by a conflict over trust, he is always on guard, expecting an attack. However, and as theorized in this book, he cannot regulate his trust system and therefore oscillates between extreme values of trust (i.e., of Iago) and distrust (i.e., of Desdemona).

The easiest solution to Othello's doubt is to ground the situation back in the known territory of the battlefield, where there is an enemy (Cassio and Desdemona) and the rules are clear: kill or be killed. In this interpretative context, where narcissistic grandiosity and paranoid conflict converge, it is quite comprehensible that Othello is led to resolve his doubt by turning his beloved wife into an enemy to be killed while ignoring all kinds of conflicting evidence. A narcissist can never be an excellent intelligence analyst, as conflicting evidence will always be dismissed to sustain the superiority of the ego and its resistance to doubt.

The play reaches its climax in the final act, in which Othello plans the murder of his wife. For him, it is a matter of all or none, similar to King Lear: "Yet she must die." This splitting is evident later when he says,

> Be thus when thou art dead, and I will kill thee,
> And love thee after.

To kill her and love her "after?" If Othello realizes that he will love Desdemona after her death, why killing her in the first place? The answer is that Othello can love Desdemona only after taking her life and removing the imagined threat of her disloyalty. Othello's bothering and conflicting thoughts are evident in the following exchange:

Othello: Think on thy sins.

Desdemona: They are loves I bear to you.

Othello: Ay, and for that thou diest.

Othello strangles Desdemona to death. When she is dying, she says, "A guilt-less death I die." Emilia shockingly finds the dying Desdemona. She asks, "O, who hath done this deed?" and Desdemona replies, "Nobody; I myself." Desdemona is an overmoralist who is ready to carry the cross even for her own murderer. In contrast, Emilia, an assertive and brave woman, exposes the truth, regardless of Iago's fury, and pays the price when he stabs her to death. At this point, Othello realizes that he has done wrong:

> Blow me about in winds! roast me in sulphur!
> Wash me in steep-down [sheer] gulfs of liquid fire!
> O Desdemona! Desdemona! Dead!
> Oh! Oh! Oh!

It is striking to realize how deep is the fracture between Othello's blind-ness and his immediate realization of his wrongdoing. He is full of guilt ("O fool! fool! fool!") and commits suicide by stabbing himself. Another case of homicide–suicide has been registered in the history of crime.

DISCUSSION

What have we learned from this play?

- For the narcissist, the loss of status is equal to the loss of love.
- As we look at each other, two different worlds are reflected.
- Doubt has a more powerful impact than certainty as it escalates our imagi-nary threats.

Now, let us dwell on the meaning of doubt and its importance for under-standing human personality. In the first part of this book, I presented the idea that our personality can be grounded in threat- and trust-management processes. In this context, doubt has two senses. The first sense is the epistemological uncertainty that accompanies these processes and the way it is taken into account. Trust, as we have learned, is always accompanied by doubt and by concern over whether a signal is one of an approaching threat. Doubt, therefore, is a part of personality. For example, the paranoid has a very low threshold for identifying signs of threat involving conspecific violence. For the paranoid, the uncertainty of a potential threat is managed through high vigilance.

The second aspect of doubt is the emotional one. Doubt is deeply connected with fear and with the feeling that we lack emotional orientation, stable grounding, and a distinct, secure, and fixed existence. In this case, doubt is associated with a freezing response and our inability to decide where to move. This interpretation of doubt appears in Shakespeare's *Measure for Measure*:

> Our doubts are traitors,
> And make us lose the good we oft might win
> By fearing to attempt.

Here doubt is interpreted not as a motivating force but as the uncertainty and fear that results in the *inhibition* of appetitive processing and its potential benefits.

At the outset, Othello can be diagnosed as having a secure base with no doubt. After all, can someone reach the position of general without having a secure base? However, the complexity of personalities, even of fictive personalities, is far beyond the basic types proposed by attachment theory (insightful though it is). Othello fails to properly deal with the poisonous doubt injected by Iago. A possible commonsense hypothesis is that Iago's manipulation probably echoes a deep doubt in Othello's own soul, a doubt about the trustworthiness of others. But the fact of the matter is that Othello *has no doubt* about Desdemona's "treacherous" behavior. He is *certain* that she has cheated on him and therefore the doubt is only a trigger that shifts Othello into a mindframe of certainty. Following this interpretation, doubt may be interpreted not only as an epistemological state of uncertainty that accompanies trust- and threat-management processes but also as a *trust-inhibitory force*. In describing Othello's trust system, we can draw on dynamic systems theory and the idea of "bi-stability." A bi-stable system can rest on only one of the two stable states. This means that, if one is a person with a "bi-stable" trust system, one can be either trusty or nontrusty. Doubt is the driving force that can change the balance of the system from the trust state to the distrust state. However, like in a bi-stable dynamic system, such a change can be easily effected only if the system is resting on a maximum point that exists between the minimum points of trust and distrust. In other words, Othello is easily convinced through doubt because from the beginning, his trust system rests on an unstable point where it can easily slip downward into distrust. Living with doubt is not simply living with the uncertainty of life but living with the full realization that doubt and its frightening emotional impact may throw us abruptly from the secure base of trust we would like to believe is solid and stable. The madman may be the beggar who believes that he is a king, but to fully live this life, we should all think like a madman who believes that he is a madman.

NOTE

1. This is a joke, of course. In the Slavic culture in which my father grew up, Baba Yaga is a kind of a witch who was used to scare young children.

Chapter Eight

Macbeth

Personalities as Formed in between People

Having been "seduced" by his wife to commit the bloody murder of King Duncan, Macbeth is tortured by guilty feelings and hallucinations while steadily slipping to his fall. In this chapter, we learn that how we observe and regulate our mind explains our personality, and why murdering your boss is not always the best option. Most important is our understanding that human personality is formed in between people rather within each and every one of us, as illustrated through the shared pathology of Macbeth and his lady.

From Julius Caesar through Othello and to Macbeth, Shakespeare's war heroes are tragic figures. Despite their glory, they seem to end their life acknowledging their imperfect human nature, which refutes all possible narcissistic fantasies. However, the first impression they create is positive and powerful. This is a dramatic effect created by Shakespeare, who first glorifies the figures and then devaluates them to create a powerful dramatic effect. We initially meet a highly impressive and powerful character but we then learn that this figure is a mask hiding a weak and fragile person. Those who believe in "thin slices of personality," the idea that we can form a valid and quick judgment of others' personalities, should carefully read Shakespeare's plays. We cannot dismiss the importance of the first impression nor its potential diagnostic value. However, Shakespeare continuously points to the gap between the facade presented by the person (his mask) and the person's hidden world (his motives and intentions). Sometimes what you see is what you get, and sometimes what you see is quite different from what you get.

Macbeth is first introduced to the reader of the play as "brave" and "noble." He is a brave general who is also a bloody figure, literally speaking, described as slicing his enemy from "the nave to the chaps." A butcher in the service of a great cause is still a butcher. The reader may wonder whether "courage," a personality trait frequently introduced in Shakespeare's plays, is of a positive and high valance. The fact that Macbeth is a brave warrior who slaughters his enemies with no fear does not imply (through the halo effect) that he is also "noble" unless being "noble" is identified with being "brave." Indeed, our original conceptions of psychological traits, such as courage, seem to be entangled with other traits (e.g., nobility) and moral values.

Immediately after this description of the "brave" warrior, we observe Macbeth and Banquo—a colleague general—traveling across a heath on their way back from the battlefield. At the heath, they encounter the famous three witches of the play. The witches represent a mirror kind of world where "Fair is foul, and foul is fair"—a world where things are the reverse of the real world. Following the work of Matte-Blanco (1975), who argued that the unconscious is governed by symmetry, we can interpret the witches as representing this realm and, as we will find in a minute, the realm of Macbeth's unconscious fantasies.

The third witch approaches Macbeth and blesses him: "All hail, Macbeth, thou shalt be king hereafter!" This blessing/prophecy, in which a war hero on his way back from the battlefield is informed that he will be the next king, is extremely flattering, as the king is the ultimate expression of the narcissistic fantasy in which one is admired. "When we gaze at each other, two different worlds are reflected," says Bakhtin, but, when the king "gazes" at his citizens, the only reflection he gains is the reflection of his imagined grandiosity.

Banquo notices that this profit interestingly scares Macbeth, who responds with "start" and "fear" to the good news. That is, almost immediately after Macbeth has been presented to us as "brave," he is described in a situation in which he seems to start as a coward! At this point, we may ask ourselves whether courage is really a personality trait. If the answer is positive, then courage should be a stable personality trait beyond time and context. It should be evident across various situations. However, the fact that Macbeth responds to the situation with "fear" clearly refutes this oversimplified theoretical stance. As Gregory Bateson (1972/2000) has taught us, stability exists at the "context" level of analysis, which means that *seeking personality beyond context is a mistake*. Macbeth is probably not a brave personality in the sense that the modern definition of personality might like us to believe. He is a brave person in some contexts and a complete coward in others. However, the contextual idea of personality is highly informative as Macbeth's various contextual expressions of courage are highly indicative in addressing the question "Who is Macbeth?" He is a brave person when encountering an external enemy on the battlefield but a fearful person when encountering his internal "enemy" in the form of his unconscious fantasies, precisely as Othello is a brave general on the battlefield and a coward when he has to cope with doubt. The conclusion is that if you are an intelligence agent trying to understand the personality of Macbeth *in vivo*, it would be wise to study the *incoherence* in his various expressions of his personality. Instead of providing your agency with a coherent profile of Macbeth as a highly brave person, point to the fact that, when he meets three witches who provide him with a prophecy, Macbeth experiences an unexplained fear, a point that should be carefully analyzed. In understanding real personalities, it is sometimes more important to understand the anomalies and incoherences than to provide a simple and coherent picture of the individual.

What has caused this brave general to feel threatened by a prophecy delivered by three old women? This is an important question if we seek to understand human personality in terms of our threat- and trust-management systems. The answer exists in Banquo's question to Macbeth regarding why he fears "Things that do sound so fair." As we have learned, in the realm of the witches, fair is foul and foul is fair. While Banquo sees only the asymmetric aspect of the prophecy, which is "fair," Macbeth realizes its negative symmetric image, which will later be revealed as his murderous intentions.

It is important to understand that, for Macbeth and Banquo, it is not clear whether the situation they have just experienced is real or not. Banquo even wonders whether it results from eating the "insane root." Seeing things that do not really exist is indeed a sign of insanity, but what has frightened Macbeth while Banquo has remained quite indifferent to the situation seems to be the way in which this unnatural situation and prophecy reflect each of the characters' own inner worlds. It is as if each of the characters has encountered his own "potential space," the intermediate space between reality and pure fantasy. Facing a prophecy concerning his own future frightens Macbeth, for a reason to be clarified as the plot progresses.

Banquo himself is suspicious of this encounter with the witches and its consequences, warning Macbeth that

> The instruments of darkness tell us truths, . . .
> to betray's
> In deepest consequence.

His attitude reflects deep suspicion toward the witches even after Macbeth is nominated as the "Thane of Cawdor" and the witches' prophecy seems to gain support. For Banquo, future telling might be a tool in the hands of the dark forces, to include (as we may interpret) the dark forces of one's own soul. This is an interesting stance, as it suggests that "truth" is not the ultimate compass for one's behavior, as it might reflect our own dark forces. Indeed,

Macbeth realizes in this situation that the prophecy is accompanied by his own fantasies of murder and that these fantasies torture him, as

> Present fears
> Are less than horrible imaginings.

At this point, he says something that is extremely obscure:

> and nothing is
> But what is not.

This is an ontological statement about what there is: Nothing is, meaning that the nothing exists, and what is, or what exists, actually does not exist. This is reminiscent of Iago's ontological statement, to which I have devoted a large interpretative section. What does it mean that "nothing is" but "what is not"? Given our previous interpretation of Iago's ontological statement, we can understand Macbeth's utterance as a psychological statement indicating the reversal of roles in the world. Naturally, what exists does exist and what does not exist does not exist. However, Macbeth reverses the roles of existence, as if he is taking an active part in the witches' world, in which symmetry reigns. Normally, we have some kind of a "contact barrier" (Bion, 1984) between the imaginary world of our unconscious fantasies and the real world. Macbeth's statement is the first hint that his contact barrier, like a defected dam, is starting to leak and that his fantasies are flowing into an area that they are forbidden to enter.

Imagination may be able to cast a dark spell over our mind where a threat can be imagined, as we previously learned. The imagined threat of Desdemona's sexual treason drives Othello to become a murderer and Macbeth is tortured by fantasies of (the king's) murder that seem to be diametrically opposed to his own sense of justice, to his own superego. Here we can first understand why the brave warrior responded with fear to the witches' prophecy. Our warrior has fantasies of murdering someone and these fantasies are "horrible" as they involve a deep *conflict with his superego*, which is the way in which we *monitor* and *regulate* our behavior according to certain moral values.

To recall, Freud has pointed out that our superego is modeled after our parents, who model their superego after society. However, our superego, like its various familial and social sources, is not a platonic entity but rather a "construct" that is always negotiated and challenged. Adam and Eve had the privilege of gaining their superego directly from the almighty but were quick to challenge it too. As we are not interested in philosophical issues, our main concern is not the status of the superego per se but rather the way people manage their relations and conflicts with their *internalized sense of justice*.

For Macbeth, there seems to be a conflict not only between his courage on the battlefield and his fear in facing the witches' prophecy but also between his will to gain power by murdering his king (his symbolic "father") and his superego which points to the wrongdoing of this murderous deed. Macbeth's threat is therefore to be found in his imagination and fantasies "poisoning" his mind, similar to the way poisonous food might contaminate the body. Indeed, the threat of contamination seems to be the major threat facing Macbeth, as it is also the threat linked with the obsessive personality, which is characterized by a punishing and archaic superego that is totally intolerant of violations of one's moral code and brutally punishes each violation.

Macbeth is not a psychopathic villain, like Iago, who plans his wrongdoings in cold blood and never regrets them. He even wishes "chance" to crown him without his "stir" or active involvement, as if his way to power could be effortless, like a kind of miraculous infantile fantasy. This is why behind the mask of the loyal general, there is another hidden mask dissociating Macbeth from his own inner wishes and conflicts. In this context, Shakespeare's interest in trust and distrust reappears.

When we first meet King Duncan, who is being told about the execution of Cawdor, a traitor who joined the Norwegian enemy, he says,

> There's no art

> To find the mind's construction in the face,

> He was a gentleman on whom I built
> An absolute trust.

Indeed, if there is a conclusion we may draw from our reading of Shakespeare's plays so far, it is that there is no simple method for finding out what is behind the mask of people, even for psychologists, and that those who pretend to be the best gentlemen, such as Iago and Macbeth, are finally exposed as the worst traitors and murderers.

However, this conclusion is highly limited in its application, as trust is inevitable and the most successful traitor is he who gains the highest level of trust through his misleading appearance. In this sense, the seeds of treason have the (potentially) best soil in those we trust most. This is an unresolved issue; otherwise, the expertise of cons would have disappeared from our society. The aforementioned conclusion is also relevant for the individual himself, as our understanding of our own personality is possible only through the mediation of others ("There's no art/To find the mind's construction in the face"), even for the person himself. In other words, there is no simple way of finding out what is in a person's mind even for a person who observes himself, as his self-observation is mediated by schemes he has acquired from the outside. If understanding other human beings is far from being a simple task, we may conclude that this difficulty is evident in self-understanding too and that this difficulty is inherent in the complexity of human personality.

At this point in the play enters Macbeth, who "humbly" declares in response to the compliments he receives from the king,

> The service and the loyalty I owe,
> In doing it, pays itself,

as if the "salary" for his courage and achievements on the battlefield "pays itself." This is of course a form of flattery and social grooming that we have already encountered in reading *King Lear*. However, this flattering statement also reminds us of the immeasurable love promised to Lear by his vicious daughters. If something is immeasurable, it has no value and is therefore meaningless. The same is true of the idea that the service of Macbeth "pays itself." In most human systems of value, there is no such thing as "pays itself." We may understand that some other value stands for the service but this value is implicit. Those who declare that their service "pays itself" are those who should worry us the most. Indeed, Macbeth says to himself,

> Stars, hide your fires;
> Let not light see my black and deep desires.

This statement corresponds with a previous statement of King Duncan, who wishes that

> signs of nobleness, like stars, shall shine
> On all deservers.

Macbeth, who is one of the "deservers," is seeking to hide or escape from these "signs" as he acknowledges that he does not deserve them. He is "hiding" from the stars, in the same way as a child who is planning inappropriate behavior avoids eye contact with his parents.

HERE COMES LADY MACBETH

Macbeth's wife—Lady Macbeth—is the ultimate villain of the play. She is the Iago, and her vicious character is immediately exposed when she is introduced to the audience. We can deduce that she has vicious plans for how to promote her husband and that she is afraid her man will not be able to complete the mission. Her reported "fear" concerns Macbeth's "nature" and the possibility that he is too full of "human kindness" to carry out what she intends. Indeed, our superego is a barrier to gaining many benefits. A person such as Macbeth who has fantasies of murder is probably not full of "kindness," so why is Lady Macbeth concerned?

Lady Macbeth, like other villains in Shakespeare's plays, seems to have a deep understanding of human psychology. In fact, there seems to be a significant association between being a villain and having an understanding of psychology. Of course, this might be an unpleasant insight for the psychologists among us. However, there is an encouraging aspect to this insight. Human beings are usually not innocent angels; instead, their libido, even the dark side of their libido, is a constituting force in a constructive activity. Judaism realized the importance of our dark side a long time before Freud and proposed, "He who is *greater than his friend, his* [evil] inclination is *greater than* him." In contrast with Christianity, which strives to annihilate the "Satan" within us, Judaism proposes to make it sublime and to use it for good. Some people, like Lady Macbeth, do not learn this lesson.

Lady Macbeth, who knows her husband, is well aware of his potential conflicts and that these conflicts might hinder the execution of their plans. He is both attracted to and repelled by the kingship, as we might expect from our theorization of the obsessive personality. Lady Macbeth declares that "ambition" cannot work without the "illness" that should attend it. This is a declared belief about the world and others, and, as taught by the cognitive-behavioral approach, our beliefs are indicative of our personality.

What kind of a personality type might hold the belief that ambition is necessarily accompanied by illness/evil? The answer, which I would like to provide as a hypothesis, is that the *psychopathic personality* holds the belief that everyone is doing wrong—or, to borrow the title of Mozart's opera, *cosi fan tutte* (thus they do all). The hypothesis that Lady Macbeth is a psychopathic personality gains support when she plans to "pour" her "spirits" (power?) into Macbeth's "ear." She actually plans to *manipulate* her husband into committing a murder that she conceives as necessary for his (and her) promotion, a murder she is afraid that he is not brave enough to commit.

Lady Macbeth's schemes raise an interesting question. Is it possible to be ambitious without some kind of "illness"? Specifically, when this concerns an ambition to increase one's social status? Ambition may be motivated by jealousy, which is one of the Christianity's seven sins (which would have been well known to Shakespeare), but what may interest us is the psychology of ambition and not its religious aspects. When ambition is evident, it is probably accompanied by some kind of motivation to challenge the same social order from which our superego emerged. Moving up in the social ladder means that, naturally or unnaturally, the chair to which one aspires will be made vacant. If this is done by force, it inevitably contradicts our super-ego, which aims to preserve and defend our social order. Guilt, as argued by Freud in *Totem and Taboo* (1938), emerges from conflict and challenges to the social–familial order. The painful conclusion is that, for a moral person, ambition has the seeds of self-annihilation as the superego conflicts with itself. For Macbeth, striving to be the king is almost trivially entangled with the bloody murder of Duncan.

We gain another layer of understanding of Lady Macbeth's personality when she welcomes her husband:

> Your face, my thane, is as a book where men
> May read strange matters.

This statement can be interpreted as her saying, "I know what is in your mind and please try to hide it from others." This interpretation is grounded in the converging minds of Macbeth and his Lady. Both of them plan to murder the king to gain the crown. For Macbeth, it is still a highly conflictual fantasy, but for Lady Macbeth, it is a working plan. The evil fantasies and intentions of the couple must be hidden under the cover of an "innocent flower" that does not show the "serpent under't." As we saw before, behind the flattering words of Macbeth to the king, there are murderous fantasies.

What is interesting about Lady Macbeth is that she pretends to read Macbeth's face like a "book." Various of Shakespeare's other manipulative villains also pretend to read other people's minds (see the chapter on *Julius Caesar*) and use the process of allegedly exposing the other's thoughts as a manipulative act. This is precisely what is described as "projective identification," where particles of the self are planted in the other for defensive or manipulative means (Grotstein, 1981). In our case, we seem to deal with a highly manipulative lady who is "interpreting" her husband's mind to move him from fantasy to action. Like Cassius's interpretation in *Julius Caesar*, Lady Macbeth's is not an objective interpretation but a manipulative act. She is taking control over the situation ("Leave all the rest to me") and our brave general is exposed as an allegedly easily manipulated, and therefore weak, character.

However, and this is a counterintuitive proposal, Macbeth actually uses his wife to recursively spur him into action to fulfill their *shared fantasy of power*. This is an important point to emphasize as the pathology of the couple cannot be simply reduced to one of them. Macbeth is a brave and authoritative person, otherwise he could not have been promoted to his position. When he submits to Lady Macbeth, he is committing a symmetrical act of projective identification where his evil intentions are delivered into his wife's responsibility.

Let us imagine a situation in which Macbeth is married to the good-hearted Desdemona, a nonambitious and an innocent dependent woman who is ready to carry the cross even for her own murderous husband. In this case, it is difficult to imagine the murderous fantasy of Macbeth materializing in practice. In this sense, Macbeth, who has not read Bakhtin and his thesis of there being "no alibi in existence," *is seeking an alibi for himself through the "psychopathic" character of his devoted wife*. Macbeth has a moral conflict with his murderous fantasy/plan. He is clearly not presented as a psychopath, like his wife and Iago, and, therefore, he seeks an alibi. The alibi removes his own responsibility by letting his wife, who identifies ambition with evil, take charge of the plan.

Personality is an act of transformation, of putting on a mask, to manage our conflicts. The dynamics of the Macbeth couple are an indication of this transformation, where Macbeth's conflict is transformed through his wife into a bloody deed. Macbeth's major threat, which originates in his contaminating fantasies, is therefore removed by depositing those fantasies with his wife. Personality is therefore not only a contextual issue but also a process of *living and propagating in between persona*. That is to say, in practice, personality is to be analyzed as existing in the interactions between people and not inside the individual's mind per se.

As Macbeth and Lady Macbeth approach the murderous deed, Macbeth is tortured by guilt. He says to himself that "bloody" acts "return to plague the inventor," that a *poisoning* cup will return to their "own lips," and realizes that his intentions are self-destructive. At this point, he decides to withdraw from his plan: "We will proceed no further." Is this a decisive decision that the plan is deeply wrong and should be given up? Lady Macbeth gives us the answer: Are you afraid, she asks, to be the same in your "own act and valor" as you are in "desire"? In so saying, she exposes Macbeth's tortured conflict between his desire to become a king and his superego. She asks him whether he is a "coward," framing the conflict as one between manhood and courage rather than of morality. Indeed, for her psychopathic personality, moral issues are of minor relevance and the main issue is one of the courage and the belief that they will not fail. Lady Macbeth exposes her cruelty and lack of empathy by saying to Macbeth that, if it had been necessary, she would have plucked her nipple from her own baby's mouth and dashed his brain out. This is a shocking depiction of a woman whose approach does not involve *care* and who believes the courage to perform a bloody deed is the only thing necessary to achieve her aim. Would she have expressed herself in such a "psychopathic" manner if she had had children? We will return later to the fact that the Macbeth couple has no children.

Macbeth cannot accept the challenge to his manhood and immediately replies "I dare do all that may become a man." This is another repeating theme in the play: the identification of manhood with courage and the courage to complete a mission regardless of the emotions involved. Again, this is another indication of the obsessive personality, which can put emotions aside to complete a mission despite its moral implications.

Our "man," who conceives manhood in terms of the ability to suppress fear in favor of a mission, cannot control his rising anxiety. The general who stood against the Norwegian enemy starts to experience visions of violence and death. He first experiences a visual hallucination of a dagger: "Is this a dagger which I see before me . . .?" At this point, he is still aware that his eyes "made the fools o' the other senses." His reason and verbalization is a barrier to the fantasy and the bloody deed, and he acknowledges "Words to the heat of deeds too cold breath gives."

Talking to oneself is a form of inner speech that activates one's superego where the superego is in its archaic form; it is a *threatening* function that internalizes threats that exist at the outside world. *When we talk to ourselves, the voices of internalized figures are brought to life*, mostly significant figures who live in our inner world. When Macbeth talks to himself, he activates his superego, which "cools down" his murderous fantasies. However, the cooling words can be silenced by other voices striving for power rather than for justice, and the bloody deed is performed when Lady Macbeth anesthetizes King Duncan's guards and Macbeth stabs him to death.

There are moments when, in contrast with our simple diagnosis, our psychopathic Lady Macbeth does not seem to be free of guilt or remorse. She reports to Macbeth that, when she observed the sleeping king, she felt that he resembled her father, and, were it not for this bothering resemblance, she would have committed the murder by herself. The image of the lady's father corresponds with the abstract identification of the father with the superego and the law, what Lacan describes as the "symbolic father." This is the internalized function of monitoring and regulating our thoughts. At the moment when Lady Macbeth is observing the sleeping king, flesh and blood, she considers whether to murder him by herself. But then, even inside this vicious woman who seems to lack any empathy, some sense of morality is evoked, but it is dismissed as such thoughts

> must not be thought
> After these ways; so, it will make us mad.

This is an interesting statement that we would not expect to hear in a caricatured description of a psychopath. Lady Macbeth suggests that dissociating our superego from our deeds is necessary to keep us sane, as realizing our wrongdoing has fatal consequences for our mental health. Lady Macbeth, therefore, is not a caricatured description of a psychopathic personality but rather seems to be obsessive like her husband. She clearly realizes the existence of morality and acknowledges the price she might pay for her torturing thoughts. However, in her mind, there are conflicting voices: some show empathy, evoked through the memory of her (loved?) father, while other voices silence these caring voices, in service of the "just" cause.

If Lady Macbeth is *not* the female equivalent of Hannibal the Cannibal, the psychopathic murderer of *The Silence of the Lambs*, why does she present herself as a psychopath? This is a very important question facing those who would like to understand personality beyond its academic scheme. The reasonable answer that I would like to give points to the transforming mask she wears to provide our brave general with his necessary alibi. In a deep psychological sense, and from a perspective that positions personality in a wider social dynamic, we can say that *Lady Macbeth is Macbeth's alibi*. The psychopathic "personality" of Lady Macbeth, which allegedly lacks any fear of the threatening superego, is therefore a transformation interpretable only in between her and her husband and probably within our general's soul.

For Macbeth, though, his wife's advice to dissociate his thoughts comes too late, as he starts to hear voices and anxiously responds to "every noise," which is an indication of the emerging madness just mentioned by Lady Macbeth. Macbeth is afraid to "think what" he "has done." Why is he afraid to think about what he has done? Lady Macbeth is not afraid to face her deed:

> My hands are of your colour [bloody]; but I shame
> To wear a heart so white.

She acknowledges her bloody deed, but does she feel shame that her heart is "white"? Is she ashamed that she does not feel any regret? Or, is she pretending to have no feelings to support her husband?

For Macbeth, facing his deed means becoming mad and "To know my deed, 'twere best not know myself," meaning that to realize his deed is so painful that it is better to be dissociated from himself. "I am not what I am," declares Iago, and Macbeth obeys the same ontological maxim by adopting a flight response, but this time from himself, as if running away from himself will distance him from the ambitious person who committed the crime.

Immediately after the murder, Malcolm and Donalbain, the king's sons, suspect that they are in danger and that they can trust no one, as

> where we are,
> There's daggers in men's smiles.

They are correct, of course, as the difference between the outside and the inside is evident throughout the play. Macbeth refers to making

> our faces vizards [masks] to our hearts,
> Disguising what they are.

This conflict between the mask presented to the outside and the real intentions known to the person is a repeating theme in Shakespeare's plays, as indicated above.

The king's sons flee from Macbeth's castle and Macbeth becomes king, as predicted by the witches. As he is afraid of the witches' prophecy, according to which Banquo's descendants will reign, Macbeth also sends murderers to kill Banquo and his son, a mission that partially fails as the son escapes from the murderers.

Macbeth is still being tortured by his thoughts and Lady Macbeth keeps trying to get him to calm down as "What's done is done," as if regret concerning a past wrongdoing is senseless. However, Macbeth keeps struggling with his torturing thoughts and concludes that it is

> better to be with the dead,
> Whom we, to gain our peace, have sent to peace,
> Than on the torture of the mind to lie.

In this statement, he actually expresses a death wish, and restates the suffering resulting from his uncontrolled imagination.

In this context, the visit of Banquo's ghost is almost an inevitable episode in the plot. Macbeth is terrified by this vision of the ghost but his wife dismisses his imagination as a "woman's story," a "painting" of his fear, and challenges his manhood again ("Are you a man?"). Again, Lady Macbeth presents herself as the iron woman, as a woman who has no empathy or regret. However, toward the end of the play, we find out that, in contrast with the profile we have built so far, she is definitely paying the emotional price for the murder.

Lady Macbeth's servant seeks out a doctor, informing him that Lady Macbeth is walking in her sleep, a symptom the doctor immediately diagnoses as "A great perturbation." This is a situation of crossing boundaries, of not being able to dream and of a realm where reality and fantasy are mixed up, as analyzed by Thomas Ogden (2003). Lady Macbeth not only walks in her sleep but also seems to be "thus washing her hands" in an attempt to remove the "damned spot," probably a spot of blood remaining from the murder, as if this spot functions as the sign of Cain. This is an imaginary spot. It is a spot that exists in Lady Macbeth's mind, a spot seen only by her superego. It is a visual hallucination that is accompanied by the hallucination of a smell. "Here's the smell of blood," she says, a smell that cannot be washed out with all the "perfumes of Arabia." Her behavior is incriminating and, as realized by the doctor long before Freud introduced his theory,

> infected minds
> To their deaf pillows will discharge their secrets.

The transformation of Lady Macbeth from a tough, emotionless, and determined woman into a mad woman is far from trivial. If personality is a stable pattern, we would have expected her to be constant in her psychopathic persona. However, this is not the case. In his reading of *Macbeth*, Freud (1916/1985, p. 303) is bothered by the same issue and writes, "And now we ask ourselves what it was that broke this character which had seemed forged from the toughest metal?" His conclusion is that "It seems to me impossible to come to any decision." However, Freud is the modest as his sensitive reading of the play hints at a possible explanation. Freud points to the fact that the Macbeth couple has no children. He explains Lady Macbeth's behavior as a "reaction to her childlessness, by which she is convinced of her impotence against the decrees of nature" (p. 305). This is an interesting hypothesis but it does not explain her motivation to commit the murder nor the collapse of this "toughest metal" woman (Freud, 1916/ 1985, p. 303).

A possible explanation is that the "toughest metal" was not toughest from the beginning and that Lady Macbeth's psychopathic appearance is a mask formed in symbiosis with her husband. A similar explanation, according to which Macbeth and Lady Macbeth are one and the same, is discussed by Freud. However, the explanation we have proposed before is that personality may be a *mutual act of transformation*. Macbeth uses his wife to establish an alibi against the voice of the superego. When this task is completed, he turns into "toughest metal" while his wife turns into a broken vassal.

The fact that the Macbeths have no children may explain their shared motivation to gain the crown as a *substitute* and defense against the threat of annihilation. Bringing children into the world is the most basic way of dealing with the finitude of life and the threat of annihilation. Gaining the crown therefore seems to be gaining a substitute through which to handle the threat of annihilation. Gaining the crown is the closet the Macbeth couple can get to almighty God and his infinite existence, and for this reason, they kill fathers (e.g., Duncan) and children (e.g., of Macduff).

As Lady Macbeth slips into madness, Macbeth prepares for his final battle against the sons of the late king, who arrived to take their revenge. Surprisingly, as his lady gives up the role of the governor, Macbeth becomes full of courage: "Shall never sag with doubt nor shake with fear." This situation supports the hypothesis that I have introduced before about the way in which personality is managed in between the couple. Macbeth even adopts Lady Macbeth's coping strategy by advising the doctor to "Pluck from the memory a rooted sorrow," as if memories, emotions, and thoughts can be simply dissected from their agent. However, while Macbeth has "almost forgot the taste of fear," Lady Macbeth reaches the bottom of her despair and commits suicide. Being informed of his wife's death, Macbeth responds with a beautiful philosophical observation:

> Life's but a walking shadow, a poor player [insignificant actor]
> That struts and frets [wastes] his hours upon the stage
> And then is heard no more.

Life, continues Macbeth, is a "tale" "Signifying nothing." Life is meaningless. Behind this beautiful poetic description of life, we can sense deep depression, the ultimate withdraw from life, the ultimate flight response.

Whenever I meet someone who speaks with me about the meaning of life, I immediately suspect that beyond the philosophical facade hides depression. Macbeth is a case in point. This depression seems to shake Macbeth's confidence in his own personal "tale," as the witches promised him that he would be safe until Birnam wood, which surrounds his castle, moves and that "none of woman born" men shall harm him. Macbeth's literal interpretation of the witches' prophecy fails, as literal interpretations are wont to do. He is surprised to see that the wood is moving. However, this is not real movement but rather an illusion created by the camouflage of the soldiers who are surrounding the castle and moving toward it. Macduff, who confronts Macbeth, was born to a woman but

> from his mother's womb
> Untimely ripp'd.

Therefore, Macduff is not really of "woman born." Macbeth is slain by Macduff, whose children he has murdered. The tyrant who strived for power as a substitute for children is killed by a man whose children he has slaughtered. A measure for measure.

DISCUSSION

What have we learned from this play?

- Personality is a process of living and propagating in between people.
- Talking to yourself is a way of activating your superego, which involves an internalized threat that works to control and regulate one's thoughts.
- Having no fear of the superego is a transformation that characterizes the psychopathic personality.

Now, let us say some words about the meaning of the superego. How do we know how to differentiate right from wrong? According to the psychodynamic approach, we internalize monitoring and regulating functions we have learned from our caregivers, who have in turn modeled them after society's norms. Threat is built into this function in two main senses. First, the superego is supposed to manage our imaginary threats, in line with our social norms. Second, just as the law is always accompanied by police, who monitor our activities and are ready to punish us for deviations by bringing us to court, we will be punished internally for ignoring our superego. Guilt, as felt by Macbeth and his lady, is an indication that a crime has been committed and that punishment is on its way. Guilt has a symbolic function too, as one of its possible etymological sources in Old English has the sense of "paying a debt." When one commits a crime, one has to pay what one owes to society. The debt is a substitute, a symbolic act, as guilt is a crime conducted primarily in one's mind. How can we pay a debt associated with a feeling of guilt? Lady Macbeth is presented to us as a psychopath who lacks any empathy, being unable to see the suffering of others. She is punished by seeing blood spots that cannot be cleaned away. Her blindness to her crime is paid for by the imaginary act of *being unable to look away*—unable to avoid the hallucination of blood. Rebelling against our superego, as illustrated by Shakespeare, is a crime that will be punished internally just as crimes are punished by the law.

In sum, in this chapter, we have gained another layer of complexity in understanding human personality. Our personality is not a personal issue but something that happens in between people. Profiling a person, or diagnosing his personality, is therefore meaningless if the synergetic aspect of entangled personalities is ignored. In addition, we have learned about the superego, which is a source of threat that does not exist for less complex organisms. For human beings, the imaginary threats that serve as the axis of their personality may be to a large extent the result of their superego, their observing parents, and the observing society that lives within us. Beyond our deepest and most abstract imaginary fears, we may be surprised to find concrete human beings, flesh and blood.

Chapter Nine

The Merchant of Venice

On the Importance of Substitutes

For Ferdinand de Saussure, every system of meaning making is a system in which value, which he equated with meaning, is formed and exchanged. Personality is our way of making sense of our and others' behavior through the management of our threat and trust systems. As such, we can learn a lot about people by examining their cognitive systems of exchange. In this chapter, we will try to understand why Shylock asked for a pound of flesh; how this act is associated with the self-hatred and anti-Semitic personality theory of Otto Weininger; and how the logic of substitution enriches our understanding of personality.

The Merchant of Venice, otherwise called *The Jew of Venice* (Mahood, 2003, p. 22), is a play I personally find difficult to read, as its main character and villain is a Jew by the name of Shylock, whose description epitomizes the anti-Semitic hate that characterized Europeans' minds for generations.

The main plot of the play is quite simple. Antonio, a merchant of Venice, takes out a loan from Shylock, a rich Jew. Antonio is a respected "gentleman" who, as determined by his status as a gentleman, holds a stoic perspective on the world, which is

> A stage where every man must play a part,
> And mine a sad one.

The sad part is clarified to the reader later, when Antonio fails to pay his debt.

Shylock shares the perspective that Antonio is a "good man," whatever that means, but confesses to himself that he hates Antonio for "he is a Christian." Is this is a racial hate per se, in the same way as the hate directed toward Othello? The answer is given a few lines later, when

Antonio, our nongentle "gentleman," humiliates Shylock in public, calling him a "devil." Shylock is aware of this humiliation and responds by saying that "many a time" Antonio has "rated me." The relations between Shylock and Antonio are therefore governed by both economic exchange and humiliation, for which Antonio does not express any empathy, apology, or regret. In fact, he promises to continue with this pattern of humiliation: "I am as like to call thee so again." This is the context in which the famous deal of the play takes place. Shylock is ready to loan the money to Antonio but puts conditions on this loan; if Antonio fails to return the sum according to their agreement,

> let the forfeit
> Be nominated for an equal pound
> Of your fair flesh, to be cut off and taken
> In what part of your body pleaseth me.

The deal is therefore very simple. If Antonio fails to pay his debt, Shylock has the right to cut off an "equal pound" of his flesh in return. This substitute of *flesh for money* is the major source of our interest, as we have previously suggested that our system of value and exchange is indicative of our cognitive schemes and hence personality. As suggested by de Saussure (1993), meaning and value are the same, and they are formed by being able to substitute one thing for another. King Lear is ready to give up his kingdom for the substitute of love and Shylock is ready to give up Antonio's debt for the substitute of hate.

How can we explain this form of substitution in which flesh is to be exchanged for money? First of all, we have to acknowledge that Shylock's motivation is not purely "economical" as he himself admits that

> A pound of man's flesh taken from a man
> Is not so estimable, profitable neither.

Therefore, we do not have here an illustration of a simple system of barter where the pound of flesh is an equivalent of Antonio's debt.

The value of Antonio's flesh can be found in Shylock's attempt to "get even" for the vicious humiliations of which he is a victim. Not only is he verbally assaulted and repeatedly degraded by the gentlemen but also his daughter—Jessica—betrays him and runs away with one of the gentlemen and with Shylock's money. Shylock therefore loses his "face," his daughter, and his money.

Why does Jessica betray her father? There is no indication that Shylock has done any wrong to his daughter. In fact, in their short exchange, he approaches her kindly as "Jessica my girl" and shares with her his agony and humiliation. Jessica, though, has a different approach to her father:

> Farewell; and if my fortune be not crost,
> I have a father, you a daughter, lost.

Jessica does not feel any empathy toward her father or any regret for stealing his money, running away from him, or converting to Christianity.

Interestingly, she is "ashamed" in another context when she wears the clothing of a boy on her way to secretly meet Lorenzo, her lover:

> For I am much ashamed of my exchange:
> But love is blind.

Therefore, we have a second exchange. The first exchange is of money for flesh and the second exchange is the one in which Jessica is transformed to [or exchanged for] a boy.

The first exchange clearly echoes the Christian symbolism in which Jesus' body is symbolized by bread. As "bread" is a symbol of money, Shylock's symbolic act is clear. In fact, the association between money and flesh is older, as in the Biblical Hebrew, the word "money" (*damim*) is related to the word (*dam*), meaning "blood" (Attali, 2010). Jews, who have been accused in various conspiracies of consuming the blood of Christians, have also been accused of "drinking" their money (i.e., blood) and literally of sucking their blood or life. In fact, blood libels, describing ritualistic murders by Jews, have in the past been quite familiar to the English imagination; the first documented blood libel originated in 1144 in Norwich, where the murder of a child named William was attributed to local Jews. In this cultural context, Shylock's substitute has a symbolic, ironic meaning relating to the way Jews were represented as a threat in the Christian English imagination. In fact, the Norwich blood libel has roots in local tales about creatures that live in the surrounding woods and prey on human beings. This is the cultural context, where an ancient *threat of predation* is turned under certain cultural circumstances into an imagined threat posed by the Jews, who are predicted as predators on Jesus' body and Christians' money. In other words, the cognitive-biological fear of predators has been transformed under certain cultural circumstances into the imaginary fear of the predatory Jews. This move involves a collective form of paranoia and projection of aggressive intentions, as has been already discussed in this book.

This point deserves further elaboration. The "Jewish" threat is woven into the fight response and its associated defense mechanism of projection. In general, the European imagination has been obsessively occupied with violence associated with the body and specifically with the issue of cannibalism, usually attributed to "barbarians." From *The Raft of the Medusa*, a painting by Theodore Gericault, to Salvador Dali's *Autumn Cannibalism*, we see a continuous interest in the subject. Interestingly, the horror expressed in *The Raft of the Medusa*, in which European gentlemen are involved in cannibalism, cannot be understood without reference to the blind spot of the French concerning "cannibalism" in its own colonies. Do you remember the boycott example that I used to explain how can we identify the mechanism of projection? In this case, too, the shock elicited by *The Raft of the Medusa* is out of proportion with the almost total indifference to other acts of "cannibalism" performed by the same culture.

Similarly, the Venetian gentlemen's disgust at Shylock's "flesh-for-money" deal cannot be understood apart from the common practices of physical punishment and the dissection of body parts that were integral parts of English society at that time. Having an unpaid debt could easily lead to the loss of one's nose as a punishment. In *Alice's Adventures in Wonderland* (Carroll, 2000), the Queen's most famous phrase is "Off with their heads!" referring to her favorite punishment of decapitation. *The enemies created by our imagination, we learn, are primarily the violent beliefs we project on others*.

The second exchange, in which Jessica is allegedly converted into a male, has a clear sexual connotation. Her exchange—from a Jew to a Christian, from a daughter to a wife, and from a woman to a man—is played out when Shylock cries in agony, "My own flesh and blood to rebel!" The flesh to be taken from Antonio is also the symbolic and symmetrical counterpart of the "flesh" (Jessica) that Shylock has actually lost.

Shylock's cry is viciously mocked by Salarino, one of the other characters, who says, "Out upon it, old carrion! Rebels it at these years?" Salarino interprets Shylock as speaking about an *erection*, and responds to the father's agony with a sexual humiliation that is followed by a denial of Shylock's own relationship with his daughter: "There is more difference between thy flesh and hers than between jest and ivory." That is, the humiliation involves the sexual derogation of Shylock as a man who has lost his manhood (i.e., is sexually impotent), and hence his manly status, and it also involves his humiliation as a father, as his biological fatherhood is suspected on the grounds that his daughter has nothing in common with him. This is a case of using the threat of sperm competition to shame and humiliate.

Shylock system of equivalence can therefore be comprehended only in the context of humiliation and revenge, as his acts, he admits, will "feed my revenge." Our Jewish "devil" is actually portrayed as a sensitive person who cannot stay indifferent in the face of humiliation.

In the most famous monologue of the play, Shylock understands that his only source of guilt is being a Jew and tries to draw equivalence between

Jews and others, the same equivalence that makes us all human beings (emphasis mine): "If you tickle us, do we not laugh? If you poison us, do we not die? And if you wrong us, shall we not *revenge*?" This individual, who is described as "A creature that did bear the shape of man" and as an "inhuman wretch" who is "Uncapable of pity," is striving to justify his humanity and to gain empathy, but fails in this mission and even fails in his attempt to get even. The devil has been defeated, to the pleasure of the madding mob.

From a psychological perspective, Shylock is a highly self-conscious and reflective person. While the Venetian gentlemen, such as Antonio, are occupied with abstract philosophical reflections, they seem to be quite detached from their experience as psychological beings, as individuals with the potential for reflective observation of their emotions, beliefs, and behavior. Shylock, in contrast, realizes that his pain results from the discrimination and humiliation of his Christian social milieu, where his basic humanity is denied, and understands his striving for revenge as a natural response to these repeated acts of dehumanization. In a deep sense, this reflective stance has an "economic" meaning that deals with exchange and value.

In his intellectual analysis of Jews and money, Attali (2010, p. 7, emphasis mine) presents a sensitive reading of the biblical story of Genesis and the deportation from the Garden of Eden:

> Thus from the human condition itself comes the first lesson in *economics*: in order to avoid *desire*, man must neither realize the extent of his *ignorance*, nor the *finiteness* of his condition. As soon as he violates one of the interdictions— by eaten the forbidden fruit—he discovers *self-consciousness* and desire, and is thus relegated to the world of rarity where nothing is available without work.

According to Attali, desire and self-consciousness emerge together from the realization of ignorance and finiteness. Moving from a state of ignorance to a state of knowledge and self-knowledge, and from being immortal creatures to being humans with lives measured (in time), we are necessarily thrown into a realm of "measure for measure." This is the realm where equivalences are formed, those equivalences on which our existence as symbolic creatures relies. The world of value, signs, and meaning is therefore deeply associated with a "narcissistic injury" in which our omnipotent and omniscient fantasies come into being, in return for a system of values in which self-consciousness plays a crucial role.

According to this perspective, desire, such as the desire for money or any other form of appetitive processing, should not necessarily be interpreted as greed (i.e., *avaritia*), one of Christianity's seven sins. Desire is the *necessary psychological consequence* of *overcoming* a narcissistic injury by turning a symbolic substitute, such as money, into a compensating object. As long as it does not aim to *replace* narcissism but reflectively functions as its substitute only, desire is a legitimate and healthy motivating force. Think, for example, about some of the extreme anticapitalist movements that exist in Europe today. These movements seek to annihilate desire's ultimate object, which is money. However, without offering a real psychological substitute, these movements may form a self-annihilating dynamic, as was evident in the bloody ideology and practices of Leninist Russia, to name just one instance.

The substitute that is therefore sought by Shylock, and his insistence on getting his pound of flesh, is not an indication of a system of exchange (an eye for an eye) nor of pure greed, but an act of revenge desperately and symmetrically launched against humiliation and dehumanization. The flesh-for-money equation, rather than expressing Shylock's own values and personality, is a mirror image of the humiliating system in which he is caught and his attempt to respond to his narcissistic injury.

Let us summarize the argument we have made so far. Shylock's major threat is humiliation. This is not an imaginary but a real threat. His trust system is such that the only thing that he can trust is the *abstract law*, specifically the law of Venice, to which he appeals to win justice: his right to gain his pound of flesh. His trust in the abstract law is indicative of a personality as well as a cultural stance. On the personal level, Shylock cannot trust other human beings, as *all* human beings surrounding him cannot be trusted. He is alone on a battlefield where no secure attachment is possible, even from his own daughter. On the cultural level, he is a member of a Jewish culture in which trust is given only to an abstract being—God—and to the symbolic law of exchange and legal law, which is the earthly equivalent of the abstract God. This system of trust involves a high level of abstraction, as it is expressed in the immaterial system of value and exchange. As Shylock is humiliated and dehumanized, he chooses the *fight* defensive response by asking for revenge, equating his own metaphorical stolen pound of flesh (his daughter and his honor) with Antonio's material pound of flesh. As an act of revenge, Shylock seeks to "get even" by restoring an ideal equilibrium between him and Antonio. The dehumanizing Shylock turns the symbolic value of money into the most material equivalence—flesh—as if he could reverse the Christian miracle (if the bread/money symbolizes Jesus' body, let us turn it back into flesh!). As the play proceeds, we realize that this move will fail. While Shakespeare's audience gains its satisfaction from observing the devil defeated, the critical reader remains with a sense of deep sadness resulting from understanding the abyss wide open on the edge of each and every human being.

DISCUSSION

What have we learned from this chapter?

• The threats created by our imagination are violent beliefs projected on others.
• Desire and self-consciousness emerge from the realization of ignorance and finiteness.
• Experiencing desire through substitutes is necessary to overcome a narcissistic injury.

Now let us dwell on substitutes and their importance in overcoming the narcissism that accompanies our existence by reading *Cymbeline*, one of the Shakespeare's last plays. In Act 1 Scene 4, Posthumus, one of the play's heroes, is describing his sweetheart (Imogen), who is the king's daughter. Iachimo, a friend of Posthumus, asks him for Imogen's "esteem" (i.e., value), and Posthumus replies, "More than the world enjoys." This means that her value cannot be specified, and to this answer, Iachimo ironically replies that the lady is either dead or "she's outprized by a trifle," meaning that her value is not so high as described by her praising lover.

The context of this ironic comment is a past dispute between Posthumus and a Frenchman about the virtues of each one's lovers and Posthumus' argument that his own lover cannot be seduced. Imogen is priceless precisely because, as Posthumus believes, she cannot be "bought" (seduced). The lady is "not for sale" and her value is, paradoxically, the fact that she is priceless.

To this idea, Iachimo responds by challenging Posthumus to bet on the value of his lover: "You are afraid, and therein the wiser. If you buy ladies' flesh at a million a dram, you cannot preserve it from tainting: but I see you have some religion in you, that you fear." As we can see, according to Iachimo, the lady's flesh can be bought and seduced, and therefore its value should not be overestimated. Posthumus accepts the bet and he is determined to prove his lady's ultimate perfection: "My mistress exceeds in goodness the hugeness of your unworthy thinking: I dare you to this match: here's my ring." Iachimo arrives at the palace and immediately starts planting the seeds of jealousy in Imogen's heart. Similar to that in *Othello*, we learn that doubt has a poisoning effect as it deeply evokes the distrust system. Imogen expresses this effect by saying,

> Since doubling things go ill often hurts more
> Than to be sure they do.

The doubt is removed when Iachimo blames Posthumus for cheating his lover by having sex with whores and urges Imogen to take her revenge by offering himself for her "sweet pleasure." Iachimo clearly lacks Casanova's talent for seduction and foreplay and, as we can see, gets straight down to business without any sophisticated attempt to conceal his motives. He is dismissed by Imogen, who is shocked by Iachimo's "beastly mind."

At this point, Iachimo exposes his attempt as a test only and praises the lady and her lover for their good character. However, Iachimo is a competitive man who cannot lose a bet, and therefore he sneaks at night to Imogen room and collects signs that could testify that he has been sexually intimate with her, such as,

> On her left breast
> A mole cinque-spotted, like the crimson drops.

Returning to Rome, Iachimo misleads Posthumus to believe that his lover has cheated on him and provides him with sign after sign until the final blow is dealt:

> under her breast—
> Worthy the pressing—lies a mole.

Given this sign, Posthumus is sure that Imogen has had sex with the Italian. Sperm competition is not difficult to evoke in men, specifically if the value of their lover is equated with her sexual exclusiveness. For Posthumus, his lover's loyalty is the center of his system of value and meaning, but, as we have learned, a center is always a *center of conflict* rather than a center of stability . . . This is an important point that we should keep in mind while trying to understand human personality.

Our system of exchange, value, and meaning concerns our innermost conflicts. For Posthumus, the conflict concerns his lover's loyalty. This is why he is so eager to bet on the issue without dismissing Iachimo's challenge and manipulation out of hand. Posthumus' response is therefore grounded in his basic suspicion not only of his lover but also of women in general.

In a monologue of hate against women, he expresses that he never knew his mother, who died at his birth, and he splits the world into devilish women and honest men. The author Alexander Solzhenitsyn—a Nobel laureate—said in one of his novels that the dividing line between good and evil cuts through the heart of *every human being*. A split mind draws this dividing line *between people rather than within each person* and Posthumus puts the cut between men and women, exposing his chauvinistic approach and his conflict of trust. Posthumus, the baby who has been "abandoned" by his mother, has no trust in women and therefore his value system—through which he describes Imogen as priceless—is actually an *indication of his innermost imaginary fears and distrust in the world.*

Pisanio, Posthumus' servant, identifies another source of conflict, which is Posthumus' low social status, which in turn is the reason the king is not ready to accept him as his son in law. Posthumus, the abandoned baby, who is of low social status, regresses to his infantile rage and pain of abandonment when he suspects that his lover has abandoned him too.

As we can see, love that is beyond measure is a meaningless and pathological love. The same is true of hate, as the anti-Semitic hate of Shylock has no measure. However, *Shylock's own hate has a perfect measure, which is a pound of flesh.* In a deep sense, the atrocity of Shylock's deal is much healthier than the boundless hate launched by Antonio and his colleagues. When substitutes are missing, overcoming the narcissistic injury accompanying our realization that we are "worm and maggot," as suggested in Judaism, or "ash to ash," as suggested in Christianity, is a process that might have fatal consequences, of which one is *self-hate.* This point can be illustrated through the case of Otto Weininger.

Otto Weininger (1880–1903) was a Jewish Austrian philosopher, a chauvinist, and an auto-anti-Semitic who converted to Christianity and put an end to his miserable life at the age of 23. He was a brilliant but tormented person who wrote a famous book titled *Sex and Character* (Weininger, 1903/2005), which was intensively used by the Nazis. Most of the book is a hymn of praise to the masculine character and an attempt to "scientifically" establish the inferiority of women. However, at the end of the book, Weininger dedicates a chapter to the Jews. Well, says Weininger, it goes without saying that women are inferior to men but there are even some races in which the men are quite far from the ideal masculinity. Surprisingly, he starts with the Chinese, describing them as lacking any ambitions (supposedly like women). Then he moves on to blacks, describing then current concerns in America that giving black people equal rights would be a dangerous move. However, the focus of his chapter is the Jews.

Surprisingly, and with impressive psychological awareness, Weininger explains that the worst anti-Semites can be found among the Jews, as *"we hate in the other what we are but afraid to be."* What is the problem with Judaism and Jews? Weininger's answer is that Jews are feminine. The proof of the feminine character of the Jews is that the "real" Jew, and similarly, women has no self and therefore has no self-respect either. If one has no self, one cannot have self-respect. Weininger, an assimilated Jew who could not find his place in Christian society and a latent homosexual who was not ready to admit his "feminine" character, turned his anger against his *personal and collective self* in an act of self-annihilation, mirroring the aggression against his Jewish and homosexual self-enacted by his society.

Racial hate, as we have learned, is primarily self-hate. *We hate in the other what we are conceived to be but are afraid to be*, and, as suggested by Attali, at the most basic level, we are afraid to realize our ignorance (i.e., uncertainty) and finiteness, the fact that our life could end at any moment.

This anxiety is compensated by self-love or its distorted narcissistic form. Self-love necessarily involves a desire, an appetitive trusty approach to life, in which substitutes play a crucial role. "In God we trust," says the motto that appears on the American dollar, but what it actually says is that we trust the substitute—money—as the substitute allows us to enjoy healthy self-love, which is always threatened by the alternative: *In God-like man we (might) trust!*

Conclusions

Our Intelligence Agent Is Getting into the Groove

And what is good, Phaedrus, And what is not good—Need we ask anyone to tell us these things? (Pirsig, 1974)

In his "Author's note" in the novel *Enemies: A Love Story*, the Nobel laureate Isaac Bashevis Singer (1972, emphasis mine) writes

> Like most of my fictional works, this book presents an exceptional case with unique heroes and unique combination [*sic*] of events. The characters are not only Nazi victims but victims of their own personalities and fates. If they fit into the general picture, *it is because the exception is rooted in the rule. As a matter of fact, in literature the exception is the rule.*

The idea that in literature "the exception is the rule" is a highly insightful comment that may explain the importance of reading literature in understanding human personalities. "In literature, the exception is the rule," and therefore literature is an artistic medium in which we can observe the exception, the unique, and the singular, being repeated over and over again, as a kind of scientific replication conducted in the author's laboratory. However, in contrast with scientific replication, literature provides us with a replication of the singular, which is banned from normative laboratory experiments, being described as "noise." Literature is therefore a unique laboratory of human "noise," one that cannot be found elsewhere.

I have described literature as the needle that stitches the abstractness of our theorization to real, messy, and chaotic life. One way in which literature stitches these two realms is by providing us with a loophole kind of perspective in which we flow from an outsider's (reader's) perspective to a perspective of the insiders, who live their life in the novel or in the play, and vice versa. In a deep sense, the experience of reading literature is like the intellectual's experience of an exile. Let me explain this point.

In his monumental novel *2666*, Roberto Bolaño (2009) presents a dialogue between several of his heroes, all of whom are academics. One of the characters is Amalfitano, who lives in exile in Mexico. Listening to Amalfitano's life story, Northon, a British woman, emphatically responds by saying, "Exile must be a terrible thing." However, Amalfitano does not agree. He describes the exile as a "natural movement, something that in its way, helps us *abolish fate*" (emphasis mine). This strange comment invites the response of another of the novel's characters, who says, "But exile . . . is full of inconveniences, of skips and breaks that essentially keep recurring and interfere with anything you try to do that's important." To this statement, Amalfitano responds by saying, "That's just what I mean by abolishing fate" (p. 117).

Our ability to experience ourselves as free individuals who "abolish fate" does not lie in providing ourselves with a convenient life that keeps us safe from the "breaks" that interfere with "anything you try to do that's important." Abolishing fate involves the experience of an outside perspective, the perspective of alienation, the perspective of the exile, or the experience of the "loophole," to use Bakhtin's term. Paradoxically, fate is abolished when we are able to reflect on our life by adopting the outsider's perspective, *despite* the "inconveniences" inherent in doing this. Reading literature involves this experience, as "getting inside" the story is actually experiencing us from the outside. This is precisely the power of literature; it enables us to gain a unique point of access to human personality.

In this book, I have proposed a relatively simple theory of personality. However, when this theory is applied to the complexity of real life, at least as represented in Shakespeare's plays, this simplicity becomes the complexity of jazz improvisation. The reason is that the components of the theory—the threat- and trust-management systems—stretch from the biological level we share with other nonhuman organisms to the cultural particularities we have developed through sophisticated symbolic systems and their deep roots and practices in various cultural traditions. Instead of summarizing this book by providing a comprehensive review of what has already been said and of what at this point should be perfectly clear, let me conclude by reading a final piece from one of Shakespeare's plays, *Much Ado About Nothing*.

In this play, Beatrice, who is the major heroine, exposes her innermost fear when she confesses, "I had rather hear my dog bark at a crow, than a man swear he loves me." Why is she so afraid of a man's declaration of love? To answer this question, we need to know Benedick, the male hero, who at the end of the play becomes Beatrice's lover.

Benedick's major fear concerns treason, as he is continuously making references to the danger of being cuckolded after getting married. For instance, "In faith, hath not the world one man but he will wear his cap with suspicion?" This refers to the idea that a cuckold's horns would be difficult to hide under a hat. Benedick is therefore afraid that his wife will cheat on him, a fear that is a combination of sperm competition and social ridicule of the husband who cannot hide his "horns" and becomes the subject of mockery. As we immediately hypothesize, he has a serious trust problem, as is clearly stated later: "I will do myself the right to trust none." Benedick even suggests that, if the worst of all were to happen to him (falling in love and getting married), then, "hang me in a bottle like a cat and shoot at me, and he that hits me, let him be clapped on the shoulder."

First, the reader should be aware that this statement seems to reflect the unpleasant historical fact that cats, one of the noble creatures living on this earth and worshiped by the Ancient Egyptians, were probably used in England as living targets to train archers. Thus, we should realize that the "punishment" Benedick requests, given the "horrible" crime of falling in love and getting married, is to become a living target. This is a highly diagnostic statement, as Benedick's risk assessment reveals the threat of falling in love and being betrayed to be so powerful that his punishing superego warns him that he might be sentenced to death (by becoming an archer's target). For Benedick, being in love implies being betrayed, which in its turn implies humiliation and self-punishment.

Interestingly, Beatrice and Benedick seem to share the *same basic threat*. This interpretation is supported by Beatrice saying: "Lord, I could not endure a husband with a beard on his face! I had rather lie in the woollen [blankets without sheets]." In commentary explaining this statement (Shakespeare, 2006, p. 178), it is said that "Ferrand (143) professes to the contrary that 'women cannot endure a man that hath but little beard; not so much for that they are commonly cold and impotent'."

Today, we are aware of the relationship between testosterone and facial hair. The statement that women dislike men without beards as they are "cold and impotent" actually explains women's preference for manly men. According to the evolutionary imperative, women may have a natural inclination to a very specific type of men who are hairy heterosexuals with a healthy sexual appetite for women. However, and in contrast with this simple evolutionary imperative, Beatrice declares her *aversion* to manly men, as such a man full of testosterone and libido may be prone to cuckolding. That is, Beatrice's fear is the mirror of Benedick's fear. In both cases, they are nontrusty personalities—one may even say "paranoids"—who respond to the imagined threat of betrayal with a fight response expressed as a continuous, and amusing, battle of wit between the two. Later, we find out that Beatrice has probably been disappointed by Benedick:

> *Don Pedro*: Come, lady, come; you have lost the heart of Signor Benedick.
>
> *Beatrice*: Indeed, my lord, he lent it me awhile; and I gave him use for it, a double heart for his single one: marry, once before he won it of me with false dice, therefore your grace may well say I have lost it.

Therefore, her distrust is nurtured by prior information, which we have mentioned as being one of the components of the trust system. Beatrice's broken heart seems to be an experience that has caused her to mistrust men in general and Benedick in particular. Therefore, given our personality theory, we can say that Beatrice is characterized by a deep distrust accompanied by a threat of treason and abandonment, which is actually a threat to status addressed by a fight response, where her tongue turns into a sword. What caused Benedick to reject Beatrice? Later in the play, he testifies, "One woman is fair, yet I am well; another is wise, yet I am well; another virtuous, yet I am well; but till all graces be in one woman, one woman shall not come in my grace."

Here we gain another layer of understanding of Benedick's personality. Benedick not only is terrified of the idea of being cuckolded but also asks for the perfect woman to have "all graces." At this point, we may hypothesize that Benedick is a perfectionist, an obsessive personality whose major source of threat is *contamination*. Women for Benedick are therefore ideals rather than human beings of flesh and blood, who are far from perfect. Recall Brutus the obsessive, who was terrified by Caesar's threat to the purity of Rome. In this case, too, we have to deal with someone whose ideal of purity and perfectness is threatened by the concreteness of life. Given Benedick's obsessive personality and his fear of contamination, it is not a coincidence that at the end of the play, and in finally confessing his love to Beatrice, "eating" is a leading metaphor:

> *Benedick*: By my sword, Beatrice, thou lovest me.
>
> *Beatrice*: Do not swear, and eat it.
>
> *Benedick*: I will swear by it that you love me; and I will make him eat it that says I love not you.
>
> *Beatrice*: Will you not eat your word?
>
> *Benedick*: With no sauce that can be devised to it. I protest I love thee.

Thus Benedick and Beatrice fall in love, surprising as it may sound, given our well-grounded theoretical analysis of their personalities.

I have used this piece from *Much Ado About Nothing* to illustrate a specific point. Analysis of personality may explain the thoughts, emotions, and behavior of Beatrice and Benedick as being organized around certain patterns of trust and threat management with all of their cultural complexities. However, the singular event in which the specific obsessive character of Benedick and the specific paranoid character of Beatrice fall in love is an event that is beyond our understanding and measure. It is this point concerning singularity with which I want to close this book.

The old intelligence agent "M." might tell us that our psychological understanding of personality should avoid the narcissistic perspective focused on omnipotence and omniscience against which I have warned throughout this book. Regardless of our theories and the enormous efforts we make to understand human beings, we must acknowledge and respect the singularities of individual human beings and the inevitable doubt and uncertainty that accompany human interactions. Acknowledging this singularity is by no means an acknowledgment that our theorization is wrong but just that our omniscient narcissistic fantasies have no place in a complex world. Understanding other people, old "M." might explain at the end of a long tutoring process, is primarily learning to live with yourself by accepting the "who" question rather than by answering the "what" question. Given this deep personal understanding, theories of personality can be of some help, and a close reading of Shakespeare may add some depth, but only when all of these chords merge into the dynamics and real "groove" of living personalities.

`

References

Attali, J. (1999). *The labyrinth in culture and society*. Berkley, CA: North Atlantic Books.

Attali, J. (2010). *The economic history of the Jewish people*. Paris: Eska Publishing.

Bach, E. (1931). *Heal thyself*. London, UK: C. W. Daniel.

Bach, E. (1933/1952). *The twelve healers*. London, UK: C. W. Daniel.

Bakhtin, M. M. (1984). *Rabelais and his world*. Bloomington, IN: Indiana University Press.

Bakhtin, M. M. (1990). *Art and answerability: Early philosophical essays*. Austin, TX: University of Texas Press.

Bakhtin, M. M. (1999). *Toward a philosophy of the act* (Vadim Liapunov, Trans.). Austin, TX: University of Texas Press.

Bashevis Singer, I. (1972). *Enemies: A love story*. Harmondsworth, UK: Penguin.

Bateson, G. (1972/2000). *Steps to an ecology of mind: Collected essays in anthropology, psychiatry, evolution, and epistemology*. Chicago, IL: University of Chicago Press.

Bateson, P. (1988). The biological evolution of cooperation and trust. In D. Gambeta (Ed.), *Trust: Making and breaking cooperative relations* (pp. 14–30). Oxford, UK: Basil Blackwell.

Beck, A. T. (1979). *Cognitive therapy and the emotional disorders*. Harmondsworth, UK: Penguin.

Billig, M. (1987). *Arguing and thinking: A rhetorical approach to social psychology*. Cambridge, UK: Cambridge University Press.

Billig, M. (1999). *Freudian repression: Conversation creating the unconscious*. Cambridge, UK: Cambridge University Press.

Billig, M. (2013). *Learn to write badly: How to succeed in the social sciences*. Cambridge, UK: Cambridge University Press.

Bion, W. R. (1984). *Learning from experience*. London, UK: Karnac.

Birkhead, T. R., & Møller, A. P. (Eds.). (1998). *Sperm competition and sexual selection*. New York, NY: Academic Press.

Blanchard, D. C., Griebel, G., Pobbe, R., & Blanchard, R. J. (2011). Risk assessment as an evolved threat detection and analysis process. *Neuroscience & Biobehavioral Reviews*, 35(4), 991–998.

Boksem, M. A., Kostermans, E., Milivojevic, B., & De Cremer, D. (2012). Social status determines how we monitor and evaluate our performance. *Social Cognitive and Affective Neuroscience*, 7(3), 304–313.

Bolaño, R. (2009). *2666* (Natasha Wimmer, Trans.). New York, NY: Picador.

Borges, J. L. (2010). *The garden of forking paths*. Penguin Audio.

Boyer, P., & Bergstrom, B. (2011). Threat-detection in child development: An evolutionary perspective. *Neuroscience & Biobehavioral Reviews*, 35(4), 1034–1041.

Bradley, M. M., Codispoti, M., Cuthbert, B. N., & Lang, P. J. (2001). Emotion and motivation I: Defensive and appetitive reactions in picture processing. *Emotion*, 1(3), 276.

Capote, T. (2013). *In cold blood*. New York, NY: Random House.

Carroll, L. (2000). *Alice's adventures in wonderland*. Toronto, ON: Broadview Press.

Cascio, C. N., Konrath, S. H., & Falk, E. B. (2015). Narcissists' social pain seen only in the brain. *Social Cognitive and Affective Neuroscience*, 10(3), 335–341.

Chekhov, A. P. (1999). *Anton Chekhov: Early short stories, 1883–1888*. New York, NY: Modern Library.

Choi, J. M., Padmala, S., Spechler, P., & Pessoa, L. (2014). Pervasive competition between threat and reward in the brain. *Social Cognitive and Affective Neuroscience*, 9(6), 737–750.

Davis, K. L., & Panksepp, J. (2011). The brain's emotional foundations of human personality and the Affective Neuroscience Personality Scales. *Neuroscience & Biobehavioral Reviews*, 35(9), 1946–1958.

Delgado, M. R. (2007). Reward-related responses in the human striatum. *Annals of the New York Academy of Sciences*, 1104(1), 70–88.

de Saussure, F. (1993). *Course in general linguistics*. London, UK: Duckworth.

DeYoung, C. G., & Gray, J. R. (2009). Personality neuroscience: Explaining individual differences in affect, behavior, and cognition. In P. J. Corr and G. Matthews (Eds.), *The Cambridge handbook of personality psychology* (pp. 323–346). Cambridge, UK: Cambridge University Press.

Dimoka, A. (2010). What does the brain tell us about trust and distrust? Evidence from a functional neuroimaging study. *MIS Quarterly*, 34(2), 373–396.

Dumas, A. (1910). *The Count of Monte Cristo*. New York, NY: Collier.

Dunbar, R. I. (2010). The social role of touch in humans and primates: Behavioural function and neurobiological mechanisms. *Neuroscience & Biobehavioral Reviews*, 34(2), 260–268.

Englander, N. (1999). *For the relief of unbearable urges*. New York, NY: Faber and Faber.

Evans, B. A., & Sheinman, A. (Producers) & Reiner, R. (Director). (1986). *Stand by me*. USA: Act III Productions.

Fouragnan, E., Chierchia, G., Greiner, S., Neveu, R., Avesani, P., & Coricelli, G. (2013). Reputational priors magnify striatal responses to violations of trust. *Journal of Neuroscience*, 33(8), 3602–3611.

Freedman, H., & Simon, M. (1939). *Midrash Rabbah* (10 Vols.). London, UK: Sonci.

Freud, S. (1916/1985). Those wrecked by success. In A. Dickson (Ed.), *Sigmund Freud, art and literature* (pp. 299–317). Harmondsworth, UK: Penguin.

Freud, S. (1938). *Totem and taboo.* London, UK: Pelican Books.

Fu, G., & Lee, K. (2007). Social grooming in the kindergarten: The emergence of flattery behavior. *Developmental Science, 10*(2), 255–265.

Gambetta, D. (1988). *Trust: Making and breaking cooperative relations.* New York, NY: Basil Blackwell.

Grazer, B., & Howard, R. (Producers) & Howard, R. (Director). (2001). *A beautiful mind.* USA: Imagine Entertainment.

Greene, G. (1938/2004). *Brighton rock.* London: Vintage.

Grey, B., Zanuck, R. D., & Siegel, M. (Producers) & Burton, T. (Director). (2005). *Charlie and the chocolate factory.* USA: Village Roadshow Pictures / The Zanuck Company / Plan B Entertainment.

Grotstein, J. S. (1981). *Splitting and projective identification.* New York, NY: Jason Aronson.

Holmes, J. (2011). Superego: An attachment perspective. *International Journal of Psychoanalysis, 92*(5), 1221–1240.

Holquist, M. (1990). *Dialogism: Bakhtin and his world.* New York, NY: Routledge.

Kaburu, S. S., & Newton-Fisher, N. E. (2013). Social instability raises the stakes during social grooming among wild male chimpanzees. *Animal Behaviour 86*(3), 519–527.

Kafka, F. (2012). *The complete stories.* New York, NY: Schocken.

King, S. (1980). *It.* New York, NY: Signet.

King, S. (1983). *Different seasons.* New York, NY: Signet.

Krane, J. D., Langsam, R., Lasoff, A., & Schain, D. (Producers) & Sommers, S. (Director). (1989). *Catch me if you can.* USA: MCA.

Kundera, M. (1988). *The art of the novel.* London: Faber and Faber.

Lansing, S. (Producer) & Lyne, A. (Director). (1993). *Indecent proposal.* USA: Paramount Pictures.

Long, Y., Jiang, X., & Zhou, X. (2012). To believe or not to believe: Trust choice modulates brain responses in outcome evaluation. *Neuroscience, 200,* 50–58.

Mahood, M. M. (2003). Introduction. In *The merchant of Venice* (pp. 1–65). Cambridge, UK: Cambridge University Press.

Malamud, B. (1963). *Idiots first.* New York, NY: Farrar, Straus and Giroux.

Mancuso, F., Jr. (Producer) & Frankenheimer, J. (Director). (1998). *Ronin.* USA: FGM Entertainment.

Maner, J. K., & Shackelford, T. K. (2008). The basic cognition of jealousy: An evolutionary perspective. *European Journal of Personality, 22,* 31–36.

Matt, D. C. (Trans.). (2004). *The Zohar* (Vol. 1). Stanford, CA: Stanford University Press.

Matte-Blanco, I. (1975). *The unconscious as infinite sets: An essay in bi-logic.* London, UK: Duckworth.

McCarthy, C. (1992). *Blood meridian.* New York, NY: Vintage.

McCarthy, C. (2006). *The road.* New York, NY: Vintage.

McCrae, R. R., & Costa, P. T., Jr. (2013). *Introduction to the empirical and theoretical status of the five-factor model of personality traits*. Washington, DC: American Psychological Association.

McWilliams, N. (2011). *Psychoanalytic diagnosis: Understanding personality structure in the clinical process*. New York, NY: Guilford Press.

McWilliams, N. (2012). Beyond traits: Personality as intersubjective themes. *Journal of Personality Assessment, 94*(6), 563–570.

Morin, A. (2011). Inner speech. In W. Hirstein (Ed.), *Encyclopedia of human behavior* (2nd ed., pp. 436–443). Oxford, UK: Elsevier.

Neruda, P. (1969). *Twenty love poems and a song of despair*. Harmondsworth, UK: Penguin.

Neuberg, S. L., Kenrick, D. T., & Schaller, M. (2011). Human threat management systems: Self-protection and disease avoidance. *Neuroscience & Biobehavioral Reviews, 35*(4), 1042–1051.

Neuman, Y. (2014a). *Introduction to computational cultural psychology*. Cambridge: Cambridge University Press.

Neuman, Y. (2014b). Personality from a cognitive-biological perspective. *Physics of Life Reviews, 11*(4), 650–686.

Neuman, Y., & Nave, O. (2010). Why the brain needs language in order to be self-conscious. *New Ideas in Psychology, 28*(1), 37–48.

Neuman, Y., Cohen, Y., & Assaf, D. (2015). How do we understand the meaning of connotations? A cognitive computational model. *Semiotica, 2015*(205), 1–16.

Ogden, T. H. (2003). On not being able to dream. *International Journal of Psychoanalysis, 84*(1), 17–30.

Olatunji, B. O., Lohr, J. M., Sawchuk, C. N., & Tolin, D. F. (2007). Multimodal assessment of disgust in contamination-related obsessive-compulsive disorder. *Behavior Research and Therapy, 45*(2), 263–276.

Parker, G. A. (1970). Sperm competition and its evolutionary consequences in the insects. *Biological Reviews, 45*(4), 525–567.

Patenaude, B. M. (2010). *Trotsky: Downfall of a revolutionary*. New York, NY: HarperCollins.

Perez, L. (1977). The messianic psychotic patient. *Annals of Psychiatry and Related Disciplines, 15*, 364–374.

Pham, M. N., & Shackelford, T. K. (2014). Human sperm competition: A comparative evolutionary analysis. *Animal Behavior and Cognition, 1*, 410–422.

Pirsig, R. (1974). *Zen and the art of motorcycle maintenance*. New York, NY: Bantam.

Roberts, G. & Sherratt, T. N. (1998). Development of cooperative relationships through increasing investment. *Nature, 394*, 175e179.

Rosenbaum, M. (1990). The role of depression in couples involved in murder-suicide and homicide. *American Journal of Psychiatry, 147*(8), 1036–1039.

Schilke, O., Reimann, M., & Cook, K. S. (2013). Effect of relationship experience on trust recovery following a breach. *Proceedings of the National Academy of Sciences, 110*(38), 15236–15241.

Schreber, D. P. (1903/1988). *Memoirs of my nervous illness* (I. Macalpine & R. A. Hunter, Trans. & Ed.). Cambridge, MA: Harvard University Press.

Seyfarth, R. M. (1977). A model of social grooming among adult female monkeys. *Journal of Theoretical Biology, 65*(4), 671–698.

Shackelford, T. K., & Goetz, A. T. (2007). Adaptation to sperm competition in humans. *Current Directions in Psychological Science, 16*(1), 47–50.

Shackelford, T. K., LeBlanc, G. J., Weekes-Shackelford, V. A., Bleske-Rechek, A. L., Euler, H. A., & Hoier, S. (2002). Psychological adaptation to human sperm competition. *Evolution and Human Behavior, 23*(2), 123–138.

Shackelford, T. K., Pound, N., & Goetz, A. T. (2005). Psychological and physiological adaptations to sperm competition in humans. *Review of General Psychology, 9*(3), 228.

Shakespeare, W. (2005). *Othello* (Burton Faffel, Ed.). New Haven, CT: Yale University Press.

Shakespeare, W. (2006). *Much ado about nothing* (Claire McEachern, Ed.). London, UK: Arden Shakespeare.

Shakespeare, W. (2007). *King Lear* (Burton Raffel, Ed.). New Haven, CT: Yale University Press.

Sher, S., Hudin, R., & Savone, P. (Producers) & Tarantino, Q. (Director). (2012). *Django unchained*. USA: Weinstein Company / Columbia Pictures.

Soltis, J. (2004). The signal functions of early infant crying. *Behavioral and Brain Sciences, 27*(4), 443–458.

Stajano, F., & Wilson, P. (2011). Understanding scam victims: Seven principles for systems security. *Communications of the ACM, 54*(3), 70–75.

Thomas, E., Eoven, C., & Nolan, C. (Producers) & Nolan, C. (Director). (2008). *The dark knight*. USA: Warner Bros. Pictures.

Twardowski, J. (2015). *The world* (J. Rybicki, Trans.). Retrieved from http://www.ap.krakow.pl/nkja/literature/polpoet/twardowski.htm

Utt, K., Saxon, E., & Bozman, R. (Producers) & Demme, J. (Director). (1991). *The silence of the lambs*. USA: Orion Pictures.

Vogeley, K., & Fink, G. R. (2003). Neural correlates of the first-person-perspective. *Trends in Cognitive Sciences, 7*(1), 38–42.

Voloshinov, V. N. (1929/1986). *Marxism and the philosophy of language*. Cambridge, MA: Harvard University Press.

Volpi, G. (Producer) & Taviani, P., & Taviani, V. (Directors). (2012). *Caesar must die.* Italy: Rai Cinema / La Talee / Stemal Entertainment.

Vygotsky, L. S., & Luria, A. R. (1930). *Ape, primitive man and child*. London, UK: Harvester Wheatsheaf.

Watkins, C. D., DeBruine, L. M., Little, A. C., Feinberg, D. R., & Jones, B. C. (2012). Priming concerns about pathogen threat versus resource scarcity: Dissociable effects on women's perceptions of men's attractiveness and dominance. *Behavioral Ecology and Sociobiology, 66*(12), 1549–1556.

Weininger, O. (1903/2005). *Sex and character: An investigation of fundamental principles*. Bloomington, IN: Indiana University Press.

Westen, D., Shedler, J., Bradley, B., & DeFife, J. A. (2012). An empirically derived taxonomy for personality diagnosis: Bridging science and practice in conceptualizing personality. *American Journal of Psychiatry, 169*, 273–284.

Winnicott, D. W. (1960). The theory of the parent–infant relationship. *International Journal of Psychoanalysis*, *41*(6), 585–595.

Woody, E. Z., & Szechtman, H. (2011). Adaptation to potential threat: The evolution, neurobiology, and psychopathology of the security motivation system. *Neuroscience & Biobehavioral Reviews*, *35*(4), 1019–1033.

Yeats, W. B. (1994). *The collected works of W. B. Yeats: Vol. 5. Later essays.* New York, NY: Simon and Schuster.

Žižek, S. (2006). The matrix, or, the two sides of perversion. In J. Weiss, J. Nolan, & P. Trifonas (Eds.), *International handbook of virtual learning environments* (pp. 1549–69). New York, NY: Springer.

Index

About the Author

Yair Neuman, PhD, is the head of the Humphrey Institute at Ben-Gurion University of the Negev, Israel. He is also affiliated with the Department of Education, the Homeland Security Institute, and the Center for the Study of Conversion and Inter-Religious Encounters. Neuman is the author of numerous papers and four academic books, and was a visiting professor and scholar at the Massachusetts Institute of Technology, University of Toronto, University of Oxford, and Weizmann Institute of Science.

www.ingramcontent.com/pod-product-compliance
Lightning Source LLC
Chambersburg PA
CBHW030650110726
47901CB00002B/643